I0901792

READING THE BIBLE WITH BONHOEFFER

Reading the Bible with Bonhoeffer
A Study in Discipleship and Courage

Reading the Bible with Bonhoeffer
9781791041670
9781791041687 eBook

Reading the Bible with Bonhoeffer DVD
9781791041717

JAMES C. HOWELL

READING THE BIBLE WITH BONHOEFFER

A STUDY IN DISCIPLESHIP AND COURAGE

Abingdon Press | Nashville

Reading the Bible with Bonhoeffer:
A Study in Discipleship and Courage

Library of Congress Control Number: 2026942507
978-1-7910-4167-0

Cover description: Features a close-up black-and-white photograph of a young Bonhoeffer wearing round eyeglasses. The right half of the cover is dominated by his portrait, while the left half contains the title and author information on a dark teal background. The title, *Reading the Bible with Bonhoeffer: A Study in Discipleship and Courage*, appears in large contrasting text. The author's name, James C. Howell, is displayed near the bottom. The design uses a clean, modern layout with teal, gold, and orange accent colors.

MANUFACTURED IN THE UNITED STATES OF AMERICA

CONTENTS

WATCH YOUR STUDY ANYTIME, ANYWHERE.

Access your *Reading the Bible with Bonhoeffer* videos and leader resources on any device with your Amplify Media account.

Get Started In Two Steps

1 Scan the QR code or go to My.AmplifyMedia.com/amplify/redeem

2 Create your free account and enter your companion code

Companion Code
JHPOD3LD

Once You're In

- Videos and leader resources saved to your account
- Watch anytime on phone, tablet, or TV
- Come back anytime at My.AmplifyMedia.com

Keep Track of Your Log In Info

Email ______________________________

Password ______________________________

Companion code subject to expiration. Code may be redeemed only by the recipient of this book. Code may not be transferred or sold separately. Internet connection required.

AMPLIFY™ MEDIA

INTRODUCTION

Ever since I woke up to the reality of the Christian faith, ever since it dawned on me that religion wasn't this or that perfunctory action or some spiritual mood swing, ever since I fathomed that reading a book besides the Bible might usher me very near to the heart of God, I have been enamored with Dietrich Bonhoeffer. I'd had at best a token relationship with God and the church through childhood and adolescence. But by God's grace, I stumbled into a group of college kids very earnest about praising God, practicing loving fellowship, and learning about Jesus.

I'd barely read the Bible, and never a religious book, until the group leader pressed into my hands a copy of C. S. Lewis's *Mere Christianity*, which enthralled me. When I finished, I asked him, "What's next?" In retrospect, he aimed way too high, fantasizing I was ready for med school after I'd stuck a single Band-Aid onto a wound: Bonhoeffer, *The Cost of Discipleship*. I bought it. Still have it. Pages worn, more words underlined and circled than not, the binding (despite my tender care) cracked, its pages almost miraculously clinging together.

About the same time, being a cynic about things religious, I read (as part of a "modern religious trends" course I was taking)

John A. T. Robinson's *Honest to God*, a bestseller hurling candid to hostile questions against traditional Christianity. He kept citing Bonhoeffer's thoughts about "religionless Christianity," which appealed to me, not being a very religious guy.

So I picked up my second Bonhoeffer book, *Letters and Papers from Prison*, aptly titled, being his correspondence from the Nazi prison camp, with all his ideas about religionless religion. But there is so much more in there that is moving, wise, brilliant, tender, and profound. Another paperback, cracked, falling apart, held together over many years by my love and appreciation for Bonhoeffer's mind and heart.

A big reason Bonhoeffer still gets so much attention is that he was hounded and then executed by the Nazis, a fact that can feel like a badge of honor or a certificate of authenticity, a mantle of authority. I'd contend that he can stand on his own and would count as a great reader of Scripture in any age or circumstance. And it's not as if he's a relic from ancient history. His best friend, Eberhard Bethge, died in 2000. Bonhoeffer's is a modern, very "now" story.

In fact, Bonhoeffer is so good that you can find yourself in something of a fan club; I've had seasons in my life I could be counted a groupie of Bonhoeffer's. WWBD? We don't really know, because Bonhoeffer wasn't an absolute rule person. He would resist laying down any firm, eternal principles. And yet we can get close to WWBD by exploring Scripture with him. We dig Bonhoeffer best by digging into what he dug! He would be amused or annoyed were we to read his books or sermons but fail to invest more time in the Bible, which sparked all he had to say.

A Radical?
A Spy and Assassin?

Two things I'd like to clarify before we plunge into this exploration of how Bonhoeffer made sense of and acted upon Scripture: First, when many talk about Bonhoeffer, even when his greatest admirers speak of him, they use the word *radical*. His was a "radical" Christianity. His words were "radically" Christian.

I am sure he would agree with me when I say Bonhoeffer was quite simply Christian. Nothing radical about being and thinking and acting upon what Christianity just is. Bonhoeffer didn't take Scripture and light some torch to make it brighter or hotter than it was. He took the Bible and Jesus at face value and didn't finesse his way out of what could not be plainer. Radical? Only when compared to a paltry watering-down of the real thing.

Second, many people who've heard of Bonhoeffer but don't know much about him would presume he was a pastor who got arrested and then executed because he'd plotted to assassinate Hitler—as if he was among a small armed group, like Cassius and Brutus planning to swoop down together to kill Julius Caesar on the Ides of March, or maybe John Wilkes Booth, Lewis Powell, David Herold, and others huddling in Mary Surratt's boardinghouse hatching their plan to kill Lincoln and key members of his cabinet in a single night.

The 2024 movie *Bonhoeffer: Pastor, Spy, Assassin*, while dramatic and moving, overplays him as someone willing to scrap his theological principles for the higher good of killing Hitler. Fortunately, the film didn't crack the top 150 at the box office for the year it was released. A handful of pundits have gone so far as to claim Bonhoeffer as a good precedent and moral warrant for the January 6 invasion of the Capitol. Whatever your political leanings, you should know that Bonhoeffer would be appalled by a violent mass attempt to overthrow the government, even his own.

When he was arrested and imprisoned on April 5, 1943, the reasons declared were his many years of defying the Nazis by speaking out against Hitler, his part in smuggling Jews to safety, and his evasion of military service. Not until he'd been in prison for nearly two years did the Gestapo connect the dots and discover his role in plotting against Hitler. But his role was marginal, limited to sharing information with the Allies through his church connections that plans were underway for a very different government in Germany, hoping to solicit Allied support.

To label him a spy? He spied on absolutely no one, nor did he poke around and swipe secret information. Assassin? He was not a member of the small circle that did attempt to kill Hitler. He'd heard of such plans, of course. Not surprisingly, there were dozens of groups in those dark days scratching their heads, trying to figure out how to get rid of Hitler.

Heroic? Yes, but not for anything he did in the sprawling, complex dreams of replacing the government. Bonhoeffer was heroic for a full decade before his arrest for fearlessly daring to name the evil idolatry of Hitler and Nazism for what it was. He spoke out, long before anybody else recognized the wickedness of Hitler and the Nazis' rise to power. It was his words that made the mighty Nazis tremble, and his words would stand if written in any place and at any time, and they have the power to speak across space and time to us today.

Reading Scripture with Bonhoeffer

In the six chapters of this little book, which I've loved writing, we'll overhear Bonhoeffer preaching, writing letters and books, and engaging in rich conversation with his friends and family. We will find that he was far from an original thinker, concocting novel ideas out of his genius. He was intellectually brilliant, but more than that, he was an unusually thoughtful, insightful, probing reader of Scripture, which explains who he was and why he did what he did.

Yes, we'll explore how to be a courageous Christian during chaotic times. We'll also ponder ever more timely questions like, What's wrong with religion? How should we pray? Why does the birth of Christ matter? Or his crucifixion? What do they mean for us? What is God asking of the church today?

Bonhoeffer's writings, and then books about him, fill about six feet of shelf space in my personal library, and he has been named in hundreds of my sermons and every one of my twenty-four books. Yet in working on this book, he has grabbed me lovingly by the shoulders and shaken me more than once, rousing me to get serious about what I'm being, thinking, and doing as a Christian and as a pastor, and has reminded me to read my Bible more slowly and carefully, expecting fresh surprises and challenges. And revisiting his home, seminary, and places where he lived, thrived, and suffered has inspired me in profoundly personal ways. My hope and prayer is that, by opening a door into his life and words, he will do the same for you.

Reading Scripture

CHAPTER 1

A LIFE WITH SCRIPTURE

As I am writing this book, Bonhoeffer has been dead eighty years. Why would such a historical figure, or any historical figure, matter today? Bonhoeffer himself repeatedly and urgently asked, "Who is Jesus Christ for us today?" How can a "today" long past impact our "today"?

William Faulkner cleverly wrote that "the past is never dead. It's not even past."[1] As people of faith, we understand how the past lingers and how people of the past aren't stuck in the past but live on in the Communion of the Saints, our "great cloud of witnesses" (Hebrews 12:1). Even Protestants are blessed by saints, the heroes of faith, whom we need more than ever in our culture that is obsessed with celebrities. The glittering, shapely, athletic, and rich strut before us, and we gawk at them and harbor a wish to enjoy all they must enjoy. We forget that celebrities feed our narcissism, our cravings, our superficial selves. Fawning over them will never make us wise or holy. Heroic saints ask something of us, like courage or living at odds with the culture.

Bonhoeffer would chafe at the way many think of him as a religious celebrity. He didn't mind being the center of attention, but he would invite us to examine with him the lives of the saints in Scripture and history.

I smile when I recall Frederick Buechner's lovely thought: "In his holy flirtation with the world, God occasionally drops a pocket handkerchief. These handkerchiefs are called saints."[2] God wooed me when I was a young adult with Bonhoeffer's life and words, which weren't anything Bonhoeffer himself invented. I hope we'll see in these chapters that Bonhoeffer was, above all else, someone who saw things we might have missed in Scripture.

Shortly after I learned a little about Bonhoeffer, I saw a photo of him for the first time—the one with those round spectacles, peering not quite directly into the camera but just so very slightly above and slightly to the side, as if he could see beyond and deeply, even while being photographed, making me wonder less about him and instead about what he saw.

Luke 2:52: He Grew in Wisdom and in Stature

Let's survey the basic story of the life of this great reader of Scripture. He was born in Breslau in Germany (today called

Wrocław and now in Poland) on February 4, 1906, alongside his twin sister, Sabine. He grew up in Berlin in an upper-middle-class family, all well educated, musical, and devoted to the Christian faith, even though they rarely attended church. A precocious, brilliant student, he always made high marks (except in penmanship!) and graduated early. He earned not one but two doctorates in theology and published academic works that would be counted as grand achievements had he not become better known for his resistance to the Nazis. He was a good athlete and tall. Why was I surprised when I learned he grew to 6'1"?

He traveled much in his short life. His family wasn't rich but privileged enough that, before his working life began, he traveled to Paris, Sicily, North Africa, Cuba, Mexico, and the Deep South of the United States. Rome thrilled him as a teenager, awakening in him a sense of the universality of the church; he was especially moved by nuns at prayer and in worship in the grand churches we tend to photograph for social media. Never was he just a sightseer. He was a keen observer of places and people, asking questions about God and "Who is Jesus Christ for us today?" in each peculiar place.

His first job was as an associate pastor in the German expatriate church in Barcelona. His sermons were more popular than the senior pastor's, and he enjoyed success in youth work. He began to notice the poor, more so once he came home to Berlin and pastored a church in one of the city's most impoverished neighborhoods.

Bonhoeffer was granted a scholarship to study at Union Theological Seminary in New York. It's telling that he traveled to the United States aboard a luxury liner! However he came, it is fortunate for us that he got here, as his nine-month stay in the

United States was a Damascus road experience for him. Bonhoeffer arrived in the fall of 1930, when the United States was reeling from the stock market (located in New York) crash, bank closures, and soaring unemployment.

After finding most churches in America to be vapid and dull, he was invited to the Abyssinian Baptist Church in Harlem by a classmate. Frank Fisher was the first person of color Bonhoeffer had ever even spoken with—at age twenty-four! The joy and focus on Jesus in this Black church moved him. He taught Sunday school and visited in the homes of parishioners. Reared as a classical musician, he fell in love with spirituals and jazz. Abyssinian's vital life of worship, learning, fellowship, and the transformation of a troubled society forever inspired his vision of Christianity.

Being far from home enabled him to understand more clearly the rising insanity back home in Germany. Reggie Williams thinks that "Bonhoeffer would not have seen the danger so clearly . . . and he may have avoided his fate . . . in solidarity with Christ, if it were not for his experience in Harlem."[3] The depth of racism in America was shocking to him and instilled in him a keen sensitivity to and determination not to tolerate the racist evil that would engulf Germany. Just as he was returning home, the earth was shifting on its axis with the tumultuous rise of Adolf Hitler to power. Bonhoeffer was the first of only a few pastors who called out the frenzy and giddy devotion to this psychopath for what it was: idolatry.

Over the next decade, as we'll see in other chapters, Bonhoeffer spoke out boldly for God and Christ and the church. He was harassed, threatened, censured, and censored. He got out of Germany to pastor a church in London for two years and was later offered a teaching position in New York. Both times, safely ensconced at a distance from the grip of evil in his homeland, he heard God's call to return, to be in the thick of things with his people, to try to stand up for God and church during the hour it was needed most—and under extreme pressure.

As faithful Christians were increasingly oppressed and as even the seminaries were pandering to Hitler, Bonhoeffer was asked to lead an alternative seminary in Finkenwalde. During his months leading and teaching, he wrote his great books, *The Cost of Discipleship* and *Life Together*. Even after the seminary was shut down by the government, Bonhoeffer continued to teach young clergy covertly for months. Eventually, he moved back into his parents' home, where he was arrested on April 5, 1943. During his two years in prison, he corresponded with family and friends. Almost miraculously preserved, his smuggled mail we can now read in *Letters and Papers from Prison*. On April 9, 1945, just days before Germany surrendered, he was hanged in the Flossenbürg concentration camp.

As we will see in the rest of this book, it is impossible to envision Bonhoeffer at any of these dramatic moments of his life without his Bible in hand. Everywhere he went, from childhood through his final hours, he was turning its pages, digesting it slowly, not hunting for easy answers but asking hard, probing questions, lingering at length over what it all meant and the One who was behind all the words. What he found there was motivation to do what he did. What he found there enabled him to make sense of what was happening to him and in the world. And being ever the teacher, he still shares with us what he found there.

1 Corinthians 13: Love in the World

Before we plunge into Bonhoeffer's harder, more dizzyingly challenging words for us, let's warm up by looking into the way he opens up some basic Bible texts that mark the passing of time in a person's life, some familiar passages we think we've understood, and see if he invites us to a deeper, more joyful place. Let's begin with a familiar one: 1 Corinthians 13.

During the season he was a pastor in London, he preached a series of four sermons on Paul's "love chapter"—without ever mentioning a wedding! His listeners were gripped with fearful uncertainty. The world was mired in an economic depression. Germans were mired in ambivalence, trying to figure out whether the rise of Hitler and the Nazis was the dawning of a marvelous new world or something sinister and even evil.

Paul's letter, like the rest of the New Testament, was written for and first read in a world where the massive might of Rome struck fear into every heart. How did Christianity manage not just to survive but even thrive in an environment where everyone loathed their rulers and were persecuted for what they believed? Why did those once hostile to the church convert?

Pondering the opening verses of 1 Corinthians 13, Bonhoeffer observed that what impressed pagans about the first Christians wasn't their ideas so much as this: "They could physically see with their own eyes that two neighbors, or a master and his slave, or estranged brothers or sisters suddenly were no longer against each other but rather with and for each other."[4] Finding themselves caught up in the seismic confusion that was Germany in the 1930s, Christians had failed miserably by knuckling under to Hitler. But their deeper failure was failure to love. Bonhoeffer envisioned God looking down on those who love and taking great pride in them.

But it's not only the other guys who are failing to love. In the struggle to be the church in such times, the great temptation is "being self-assured, self-righteous and dogmatic, that is, the temptation to be unloving toward one's enemy. And yet this enemy can never truly be overcome except by love."[5] Jesus never eases up on this necessity to love our enemies.

As we'll see later, Bonhoeffer had much to say about love as the situation worsened in World War II Europe. In 1934, he was preaching to people sorely divided, with rising rancor toward their fellow German citizens who thought wrongly about politics. Sound familiar?

Just as Paul had written that love is patient, kind, never arrogant or rude, that love does not insist on its own way, and that it bears all things, Bonhoeffer spoke to his parishioners—and to us: "Even when the other person turns out to be sinful and spiteful, love does not become bitter, because it is not looking to receive kindness. It is thinking not of itself at all but only of the other. It grieves over the other's nastiness, is saddened by it, and loves him or her all the more."[6] We may well ask ourselves as Christians and as a church—your church even—Are we loving out there in public? Or passing judgment? Do we try to be the world's moral police, or are we known for our love? When will we see another Martin Luther King Jr., who spoke of love in the public square and about political issues?

I love Bonhoeffer's reflection (literally!) on "Now we see in a mirror dimly." Did he spend time looking into a mirror as he prepared his sermon?

> The thoughts of God are only seen in the world as if reflected in a mirror. We see them only as if in mirror writing. And God's mirror writing is hard to read. It says that the great is small and the small is great, that right is wrong and wrong is right, that a promise awaits the hopeless while judgment awaits those who are full of hope; it says that the cross signifies victory and death signifies life. We can read God's mirror writing in Jesus Christ.

Now I see what I would never have seen had he not seen.

During seasons of intense political and economic turmoil (and, truth be told, even during times of prosperity and calm), well-meaning Christians have this habit of mixing up what is good and what isn't, what is of God and what isn't. Bonhoeffer named the problem and offered up the mirror in which we see and then know what to do: it's Jesus, not the Jesus of our self-indulgent invention, but the one in Scripture. Bonhoeffer, at every turn, was careful to add "Jesus alone," or "only Christ," a not-so-subtle reminder that in 1934, Germans were fawning over another leader (a Führer) spouting fake truths with evil tucked inside.

Psalm 90: His Grandmother's Funeral

When Bonhoeffer preached his series on 1 Corinthians 13, he could speak not only of our public responsibility to love. He had enjoyed growing up in a marvelous, profoundly close, loving family, which he probably had in mind when, in the first sermon, he wrote, "Human life is only meaningful and worthwhile to the extent that it has love in it. . . . A life is worth as much as the love in it." And then he alluded to what it's like to stand at the grave of someone who did not love much and was not loved much, contrasting this with standing at the grave of one much beloved who'd loved much.

As he spoke, his grandmother was in her final months of life. Remarkably, in her nineties, she defied Nazi boycotts of Jewish businesses, pushing past armed soldiers to buy fruit from a Jewish merchant. When she passed away, Bonhoeffer preached at her grave from Psalm 90, a text read every New Year's in the Bonhoeffer household. I visited her grave—by chance!—on the ninetieth anniversary of her funeral. It was sixteen degrees, with snow and ice all over the ground. I pictured Bonhoeffer and his family, amid the chill, pondering this psalm, which asks questions like, What is the value of a life? "It is with enormous gratitude that we stand today at the grave of our dear deceased grandmother. God's hand extended its beneficence to us by allowing her to live with us until today."[7] He spoke of her good cheer in the face of troubles, her wisdom, and that she made yet one more Christmas at age ninety-three.

The psalm's opening line? "God is our refuge." God had been her refuge when her father died young, as did two sons, and then three grandsons in World War I. The psalm meditates on the long passing of time and what remains. Bonhoeffer's grandmother "mediated to us the inheritance of a different time"—a lovely thought, not that we inherit things but times long past. "With her, we are losing a world that all of us, in one way or another, bear within us and indeed want to bear within us. The uncompromising nature of justice, the free word of the free person." Can you hear his subtle jab at the toxic German world of that day? He named her anguish over the Jews. "She came from another age, from another spiritual world, and this world does not go down into the grave with her. This inheritance, for which we are grateful to her, obligates us." What "lingering obligations" come our way at a funeral?

And finally, he riffed on the psalm's plea to "number our days." We all have some boundary. As God is beyond that boundary, we live now with courage as we labor for God in the world. Bonhoeffer, not quite thirty years old as he stood at her grave, could not have guessed that the number of days he had left was 3,372, quite a few in one way, but less than a decade.

He would die far too young, just thirty-nine years old, one of an astonishing crowd of God's best ones who died at thirty-nine, including Martin Luther King Jr., Frederic Chopin, Flannery O'Connor, Blaise Pascal, the Bible's King Josiah, Malcolm X, Amelia Earhart, Cleopatra, and Dylan Thomas, among others. We'll think together more about Bonhoeffer's own dying in chapter 6. For now, he's showing us that where you're standing when you read a text matters. What time it is—in the world, and in your life—impacts how you read and understand.

Ephesians 5:14: Baptism of His Nephew

From the end of life, let's turn to its beginning. Bonhoeffer preached a brief, eloquent homily for the baptism of his nephew, Friedrich, in 1932. What intrigues me is his choice of text. We might expect something like Matthew 19:14, "Let the children come to me." But instead, Bonhoeffer surprisingly chose Ephesians 5:14, "Sleeper, awake! Rise from the dead, and Christ will shine in you." In a way, newborns are waking from their warm, comfortable slumbers in the mother's womb. Given the perils of the day, no thinking pastor could issue sweet words of comfort, as if God would protect this child. The waking up for the child and parents meant they must be realistic, but not afraid, for God is still God. No wonder Bonhoeffer cited "Sleeper awake!" when explaining how grown-ups are to begin each day: we wake and are silent, listening for God who made the day to have the first word.

Far darker was the day the newborn son of Bonhoeffer's closest friend, Eberhard Bethge, was baptized. May 1944: Jews were being gassed in death camps; German cities were bombed out as the war was surely lost but still raging. Most shocking and appalling is this: The Nazis had begun to require that all baptisms include the prayer "that this child will grow up to be like Adolf Hitler and Heinrich Himmler." We can be sure the Bethges refused to comply.

They'd named the boy Dietrich, but Bonhoeffer was in seclusion in the Tegel prison. The news of the birth and scheduled baptism was smuggled in to him, and he had to hock his watch to smuggle a letter out to the Bethges—a marvelous, hopeful, downright joyful message of blessing over his namesake, with not a hint of self-pity or sadness.

Bonhoeffer's words might surprise us, but they were essential in such a nation like Germany—and perhaps in every place and time! In baptism, there is a "break with the world" that is "absolute." It really is a kind of death, the word we hear in the baptismal liturgy but hardly notice. The child, the family, and the church pledge to die to this world and its idolatries and sin. Serious stuff, a far cry from many families I barely know dressing up and materializing in church to (as one dad put it to me) "get the baby done."

He ended his long message thus: "You are being baptized today as a Christian. All those great and ancient words of the Christian proclamation will be pronounced over you . . . without your understanding any of it."[8] Even as the church was fighting for survival, Bonhoeffer declared that survival would be pointless if, in surviving, the church forgets reconciliation, redemption, love of enemies, cross and resurrection, and discipleship. Baby Dietrich would meet and know family born in the 1800s but would himself probably live to the year 2000. He would be "a living bridge," perhaps playing a role in the recovery of the spirit of olden times on the verge of being lost during the terrible cataclysm of the war.

Jeremiah 32: Engagement to Maria

Bonhoeffer had no children. He didn't show a lot of interest in girls or then young women, prompting some to conclude he was gay, especially given his intense friendship with Eberhard Bethge. This would be, to me, the least interesting question we could raise about him. Our curiosity about whether he was gay or not might reveal something unwell in our souls. I also wonder if in sizing up others as either straight or gay, we miss lovelier possibilities.

I think of Jonathan and David: First Samuel 18:3 tells us "Jonathan loved David as his own soul," and when Jonathan died, David lamented, "I am distressed for you, my brother Jonathan;

very pleasant have you been to me; your love to me was wonderful, passing the love of women" (2 Samuel 1:26). Can't it be that David and Jonathan, and Dietrich and Eberhard, and a great many same-gender relationships are exceptionally close and intimate and yet not sexual?

We do know that in June 1942, at the age of thirty-six, he met young Maria von Wedemeyer, whose grandmother had funded Bonhoeffer's work in Finkenwalde. Pretty quickly, Dietrich and Maria were engaged to be married—and then only a few weeks later, he was arrested. His correspondence with her is simply lovely, replete with tender expressions of love and longing, and a fair bit of poetry.

Always the theologian, Bonhoeffer sensed not just his good fortune but God's "special guidance," and "a token of God's grace and goodness"[9] in bringing them together so shortly before his arrest and imprisonment. Bonhoeffer was simply unable to process his life without discerning its meaning and purpose in Scripture, even his engagement—and so his letters to Maria turned to Scripture.

Mind you, I have occasionally tried my hand at quoting Bible in my relationship with my bride. A couple of times, maybe a Valentine's Day or our anniversary, I read to her, in my most romantic voice, these words from God's word: "You are beautiful! Your eyes are doves behind your veil. Your hair is like a flock of goats moving down the slopes of Gilead. Your teeth are like a flock of shorn ewes. . . . Your cheeks are like halves of a pomegranate. . . . Your neck is like the tower of David" (Song of Solomon 4:1-4). I wish I could report that she was swept off her feet.

In Bonhoeffer's case, he draws Maria's attention to the prophet Jeremiah, who was instructed by God to purchase a field to farm, just days before the Babylonians were sure to conquer and destroy the land of Judea on which it sat (Jeremiah 32). He writes,

> When I consider the state of the world.... When Jeremiah said, in his people's hour of direst need, that "houses and fields (and vineyards) shall again be bought in this land," it was a token of confidence in the future. That requires faith... the faith that endures in the world and loves and remains true to that world in spite of all the hardships it brings us. Our marriage must be a "yes" to God's earth. It must strengthen our resolve to accomplish something on earth.

Jeremiah's purchase and their engagement were bold, seemingly crazy commitments to a future in the face of all but impossible odds. And Bonhoeffer didn't go spiritual on Maria (or us). It is on and for this earth that Jeremiah hoped, and that Bonhoeffer hoped. He concluded with a touch of humor: "I fear that Christians who venture to stand on earth on only one leg will stand in heaven on only one leg too." But as we will see in chapter 5, Bonhoeffer's is always a Christianity with its feet firmly standing on this earth.

1 Corinthians 2:7-10: Divine and Human Mystery

Even though Bonhoeffer didn't have much dating experience, his was a soul peculiarly attuned to what's needed in any relationship. He amazes me at every turn with his depth of insight—and at an early age. In a sermon he preached on 1 Corinthians 2:7-10 when he was just twenty-seven years old, he opened by naming our fear and misunderstanding of mystery, as if it's something secretive, something we'd best figure out soon. Mystery is wonder and curiosity and delight; the spiritual life is all about getting a glimpse of a marvel and then being humbled yet enchanted, delighting in what is inexhaustible, a sumptuous uncharted world to explore.

Riffing on Scripture's many references to mystery, Bonhoeffer preached the following—and I try to picture his congregation as their jaws dropped in amazement:

> Mystery...does not mean simply not knowing something. The greatest mystery is not the most distant star; on the contrary, the closer something comes to us and the better we know it, then the more mysterious it becomes for us. The greatest mystery to us is not the most distant person, but the one next to us. The mystery of other people isn't reduced by getting to know more and more about them. Rather, in their closeness they become more and more mysterious. And the final depth of all mystery is when two people come so close to each other that they *love* each other.... When two people know everything about each other, the mystery of the love between them becomes infinitely great.... Knowledge about each other does not remove the mystery, but rather makes it more profound.[10]

I did not understand this aspect of love when I was younger. But realizing it now, as I walk through life with my spouse, my children, and my friends, this sense of mystery is freeing, even joyful. I'm a better listener, a more keen observer. Control is something I don't attempt so often. And because of this, I am coming to a richer understanding of God and the life of faith, which is deepened by curiosity and resting in what I can't know or fix or manage. Bonhoeffer's actions and then his composure, his courage, and his wisdom had to have been birthed from some gyroscope in his soul that kept his attention trained on the God he knew and didn't yet know, realizing outcomes were unpredictable and uncontrollable, mysteries all.

Matthew 17:1: Jesus Led Them up on a High Mountain

While writing this book, I traveled to places that mattered in Bonhoeffer's life and development. In Barcelona, he would climb up to Tibidabo, a mountain overlook, and ponder Bible moments set on high places. In Rome, he scaled the Spanish steps to Trinità dei Monti with its spectacular view of so many church domes, prompting him to exclaim, "Magnificent!"[11] Wisdom is a matter of perspective, of getting out of the weeds and assuming God's larger view. Business guru Ronald Heifetz suggests leadership is about getting off the dance floor and viewing things from up in the balcony. How many of the Bible's transformative moments happened at a high place?

Such a perspective is a matter of not only place and distance but also time. Between Christmas and New Year's, at the end of 1943, Bonhoeffer wrote a long, profound letter to his close circle of friends. *Letter* might be the wrong word. "After Ten Years" is eighteen pages in *Letters and Papers from Prison* and is more of a declaration of faith, an assessment of what he and his wider circle have learned over the past decade. To do such a thing, he suggests, is "a part of responsible living." His insights, from the paradoxical height of his prison cell, tell us much of what we'd best understand if we are to be faithful in a world of troubles and evil.

Those original pages of "After Ten Years" have their own great story. When the Gestapo arrived at the house to arrest Bonhoeffer, he quickly hid those pages in the rafters of his upstairs bedroom before they made it up the stairs. When they searched the room, they (thankfully) didn't find them. A blessing for us.

> Who stands fast? Only the one whose ultimate standard is not his reason, his principles, conscience, freedom, or virtue; only the one who is prepared to sacrifice all of these when, in faith and in relationship to God alone, he is called to obedient and responsible action. Such a person is the responsible one, whose life is to be nothing but a response to God's question and call.[12]

"Whoever despises another human being will never be able to make anything of him. Nothing of what we despise in another is itself foreign to us" (words written during a season of so much despising!). And then he believes, with impressive optimism, that even in the dark days of this awful war, there is "a new sense of nobility being born that binds together a circle of human beings drawn from all existing social classes. Nobility arises from and exists by sacrifice, courage, and a clear sense of what one owes oneself and others, and naturally shares a natural regard for others." What would you say you've learned about God and discipleship over the past decade?

Wisdom is in learning, in realizing what you don't yet know, or what you haven't gotten right just yet. Saints or heroes never burst into the world fully formed. Bonhoeffer had his struggles and changed his mind about important things. As a young pastor in Barcelona, he sounded like a Christian Nationalist; later, he so regretted things he said about prioritizing Germany's success above the simple demands of Jesus. In 1935, an invitation to teach in New York provided him the chance to escape Germany, which most would have seized. But on the ship coming over, he was already in turmoil, fearing he'd made a mistake. Reflecting on Revelation 3:11 ("I am coming soon; hold fast"), he stayed only twenty-six days before hurrying home, returning to the fray.

Then there was the incident of the funeral of his twin sister Sabine's father-in-law, William Leibholz, who was Jewish. Bonhoeffer agonized and dithered and finally sought counsel from his superintendent in the Lutheran Church, who sternly cautioned him against conducting such a service, fearing it would stir up a brouhaha and increase trouble for Bonhoeffer and the church. And so he declined. A few months later, he wrote a painful letter to Sabine, pleading with her to forgive him, tormented as he was by his weakness. He had not yet figured out how to be as brave as his grandmother.

Personally, I take some paradoxical comfort that even Bonhoeffer could write, late in his life, "I am guilty of uncontrolled desire. I am guilty of cowardly silence at a time when I ought to have spoken. I am guilty of hypocrisy and untruthfulness in the face of force. I have been lacking in compassion and I have denied the poorest."[13] He even had some qualms about his own bestselling book, *The Cost of Discipleship*. I love that Bonhoeffer was, like all of us, finding his way, learning until the very end from missteps and flawed thinking.

Why does a historical figure matter? Why does any life matter? Sometimes, what we discover in the heart of someone in the past who weathered storms that we are sure would crush us is a thought, a mood, or a disposition that actually helps us, liberating us from some of the superficial normalcy that settles around us like dust. Twenty-four days before Christmas, the holiday he'd always delighted in so much, he wrote a letter to Maria that opens a window into what really matters and what simply doesn't:

> I think we're going to have an exceptionally good Christmas. The very fact that every outward circumstance precludes our making provision for it will show whether we can be content with what is truly essential. I used to be very fond of thinking up and buying presents, but now that we have nothing to give, the gift God gave us in the birth of Christ will seem all the more glorious; the emptier our hands, the better we understand what Luther meant by his dying words: "We're beggars, it's true." The poorer our quarters, the more clearly we perceive that our hearts should be Christ's home on earth.[14]

Matthew 16: Who Do They Say I Am?

Sorting through what matters and what doesn't really helps us come to terms with ourselves. My identity isn't wrapped up in things or successes or circumstances or even location—and certainly not in what others think about me. Not long before his execution, Bonhoeffer wrote a poem that is often quoted by people who don't know much else about him. "Who Am I?" is its title. In the solitude of his prison cell, he has something of a conversation with himself, one that reminds me of Jesus asking his disciples, "Who do people say that I am?" (Mark 8:27).

How fascinating for us to listen to and think about Bonhoeffer now, to hear him, from prison, ask, "Am I really what others say of me? Or am I only what I know of myself? Restless, yearning, sick, like a caged bird, struggling for life breath?"[15] He reports his yearning for flowers and the voices of birds and of his deep thirst for human voices, especially words of kindness. He prays in this dreary place, yes, but it feels "weary and empty." Without trying hard, we feel some measure of his loneliness and agony. At the poem's ending, he asks again, "Who am I? This one or the other?" His answer, doggedly clinging to faith in this place of despair? "Whoever I am, thou knowest me; O God, I am thine."

We read the Bible with Bonhoeffer not to collect little nuggets of spiritual insights from him or simply to know more about another great Christian. Instead, we follow him into the pages of Scripture he treasured, which ultimately took him to the place where, in the direst circumstances and the thickest of uncertainty, he could answer the question, "Who am I?" with "You know, O God, I am yours." Notice he doesn't claim any great faith or piety or goodness about himself. It's all God. He simply is God's. The goal of our study? It is this assurance, this truth that is true even if you doubt it or don't even care any longer. You are God's. That's how your life matters, as Bonhoeffer's did.

Chapter 2

WHO IS JESUS CHRIST TODAY?

Dietrich Bonhoeffer was an academic titan in the field of theology. And yet, what he had to say about God is alarmingly simple, direct, and accessible. And he understood well that our take on who God really is determines everything else, not just in our religious lives but in all of life in this world. Bonhoeffer's thinking about God never has a dusty, old museum feel. His pressing question, always, was, Who is Jesus Christ today?

Exodus 32: No Other Gods

Shortly after Hitler seized power in 1933, Bonhoeffer preached a brilliant sermon on a Bible passage that could not have been more fitting, Exodus 32: Moses on the mountain with God, the people down in the valley, impatient and perverse, crafting a golden bull, led by no stranger but Moses's own brother, Aaron. Bonhoeffer asks why Moses and Aaron, siblings, couldn't stick together. Why do we wind up with "the church of Moses and the church of Aaron, the church of the Word and the church of the world, always breaking apart?"[1]

Bonhoeffer finds the reasons for the Israelite debacle at Mount Sinai, and for the shameful perversion of the church in Germany, in Exodus 32. The people want results. They want achievements for their nation and they want them now. They don't wish to be rid of religion. They want religion, but one that suits their fantasies, whatever will serve them and serve them now, instead of the true God. Those jittery Israelites fashioned as their god the kind of mighty beast they dreamed God would be for them, the kind of beast they dreamed of being themselves.

With impressive insight, Bonhoeffer probes what lies beneath such foolish turns toward what is fake. "The human race is ready to make any sacrifice that allows it to celebrate itself, to worship its own accomplishments." I'd not thought of it this way before, but yes, they replace Moses's invisible God up in the clouds with a god of their own making. And they spend lavishly on that god, and then "the people blissfully fall down and gaze at the idol they have created." Similarly, in the streets outside that church in Berlin, people were giddy with dogged delight over their pompous Führer.

But Moses comes down to do what Bonhoeffer and a small handful of other brave clergy were doing in Germany: "brandishing high in his hands the tablets of the law, so that everyone must see the writing engraved on them by the hand of God: 'I am the Lord your God, you shall have no other gods before me!' "

Who, for Bonhoeffer, was this God? What does Bonhoeffer have to say to us about the person, the character, and the activity of God in Jesus Christ? Bonhoeffer would nod appreciatively that we began this chapter with an Old Testament text, and we will weigh his thoughts on others as we proceed. Late in his life, he wrote a much-quoted letter to his friend Eberhard that moves me deeply:

> My thoughts and feelings seem to be getting more and more like those of the Old Testament, and in recent months I have been reading the Old Testament much more than the New. It is only when one knows the unutterability of the name of God that one can utter the name of Jesus Christ; it is only when one loves life and the earth so much that without them everything seems to be over that one may believe in the resurrection and a new world; it is only when one submits to God's law that one may speak of grace; and it is only when God's wrath and vengeance are hanging as grim realities over the heads of one's enemies that something of what it means to love and forgive them can touch our hearts. In my opinion it is not Christian to want to take our thoughts and feelings too quickly and too directly from the New Testament.[2]

He's reflecting on the way Jews do not utter the holy name of God aloud for fear of taking it in vain. He also notes that the Old Testament shows little to no interest in life after death, that laws come from God, and that wrath is a reality. When Bonhoeffer speaks of God, and even when he speaks of Jesus Christ, he does so holding both testaments closely together.

Matthew 16:13-28: Who Is Jesus Christ Today?

As a junior lecturer (just twenty-seven years old) at the University of Berlin, he declared "Teaching about Christ begins in silence. . . . The church's silence is silence before the Word."[3] It's not what we know or think we know or have figured out about God, or even what we think we need from God, that matters. We begin by listening. Before we speak, we hear what has been revealed to us.

And we always measure whatever gets said about God in Jesus Christ by what we hear in Scripture. Just because someone is talking about Jesus, even if it's a superbly educated, well-published theologian, doesn't mean we should listen. Noting the way all Christians either deal directly with the real Jesus or evade him, Bonhoeffer, thinking of pastors and seminary professors who were *Heil*-ing Hitler, vividly warns us: "The theologian makes the same attempts to encounter Jesus or get round him. Theologians betray him and simulate concern. Christ is always betrayed by the kiss. . . . There are only two possibilities of encountering Jesus: either man must die or he kills Jesus."

Strong language here! The dying he mentions is dying to your old self, to your preconceived notions of who Jesus is and what he asks of us. Of course, physical death was what pastors like Bonhoeffer risked in daring to breathe even a word questioning Hitler. In the face of tyranny and turmoil, identifying God correctly and exposing whoever pretends to be God but is not are of utmost importance, matters of life and death.

Hitler was "a master of disguise, presenting himself as a person and a politician who maintained firm religious beliefs and was committed to defending the values of Christianity."[4] Privately, though, he told his inner circle in 1937, "We will have to bend the churches to our will and make them serve us.... We will have them eating out of our hands." Overflowing with ridicule for the religion he despised, he declared, "We need to get to the point where only idiots stand behind the pulpit and only old women sit in front of it." He cast his politics, as all dangerous politicians do, as if it were a religion, with sermons, songs, liturgies, and processionals, demanding the kind of loyalty and zeal only a true God should ask for.

Understanding all that was at stake, Bonhoeffer mastered this task of answering Jesus's question, "Who do you say that I am?" (Matthew 16:15) while at the same time refusing, like Daniel, Shadrach, Meshach, and Abednego of old, to bow down to the impressive, successful but fake and false god of the day. Even if he had lived during other days in some other place, Bonhoeffer would be regarded as one of our great theologians. Fans love to characterize his thinking and his life as "radical" Christianity, but it is truer simply to realize his theology is simply Christian, period. His theology only seems radical because the vast majority around him had veered off from the basics, succumbing to the allure or the pressures of the Nazi tidal wave.

As a way to reflect on his theological reading of Scripture, we can categorize his most impassioned thoughts about God under just three words: *Child*, *One*, and *Suffering*. Let's begin with Bonhoeffer's lovely ways of talking about God-as-Child.

Isaiah 9:6: Unto Us a Child Is Born

The Bonhoeffer family had always made a big deal out of Christmas. Dietrich's richest letters from prison were written during those December days leading up to Christmas. He certainly missed family and festivities. But he also had a firm grasp on why Christmas matters so much theologically. Protestants fix their attention on Holy Week, especially Good Friday and Easter—and not wrongly! But God's saving action, God's redemption of us and the world, isn't just cross and resurrection. It's also Incarnation, the Word made flesh, Immanuel ("God with us"), God becoming one of us so we might become like God.

Let's listen to how Bonhoeffer talks about Advent, Christmas, the birth, and God coming among us. In a Christmas message in 1939 to the Confessing Church pastors, a dwindling and much-imperiled collection of the faithful, he writes, "No priest, no theologian stood at the cradle of Bethlehem. And yet all Christian theology finds its origin in the miracle of miracles, that God became human." Indeed, all sacred theology "originates in prayerful kneeling before the mystery of the divine child in the stable." He reminds them and us that theology, preaching, and teaching aren't tasked with solving the mystery of God; our task is "to keep the miracle of God as miracle, to comprehend, defend, and exalt the mystery of God, precisely as mystery."[5]

His beloved text when meditating on the glory of God as the Christ Child? Isaiah 9:6—which I cannot read without hearing in my head the mighty chorus from Handel's *Messiah*: "For unto us a child is born . . . and his name shall be called Wonderful Counselor, Mighty God, Everlasting Father, Prince of Peace."[6] I wrote a whole book on this text,[7] and my take is a bit different from Bonhoeffer's in terms of history and timeline. I point out that Isaiah spoke these words to the Israelites in a dire crisis some seven hundred years before Christ. Isaiah is not predicting a child would come in seven centuries (which would not have been any help to them with the Assyrian armies bearing down on Jerusalem!), but he's pointing to a child born in the royal household right then. The child's given name in that moment, Immanuel, God with us—and then Wonderful Counselor, Mighty God, Everlasting Father, Prince of Peace. Those names were like a sermon to the people, stirring trust in God during their darkest hours. Once Jesus came, that ancient name, Immanuel, fit what God was ultimately up to in becoming the child of Mary.

Bonhoeffer puts a different spin on that time gap of seven centuries. "The prophet is so deeply immersed in God's thoughts and decrees that he speaks of what is to come as if he has already seen it. . . . What will take place someday is already real and certain in God's eyes."[8] So Bonhoeffer sees Isaiah as mystically perceiving the birth of the Messiah in the far distant future. To anyone skeptical about this possibility, Bonhoeffer nods and yet counters: "How are we who do not know what will happen next year supposed to understand that someone can look forward many centuries? . . . Only the Spirit of God can pull this off!"

Why does God's arrival not as a mighty warrior but as a vulnerable child matter—for Bonhoeffer or for us? "God does not want people to be afraid."[9] No one is afraid of a newborn. And yet doesn't a newborn command a room? "His poverty in the manger is his might." To know God, and to know how to live with and for God, we linger at the manger. "How shall we deal with such a child? Have our hands, soiled with daily toil, become too hard and too proud to fold in prayer at the sight of this child? Has our head become too full of serious thoughts?" Bonhoeffer, in a mood as gentle and generous as that of a newborn, invites us to bring our stresses and our struggles, and even "our sense of importance" before this child, "bowing before the divine child in the manger like children."

How fascinating that Bonhoeffer could think so tenderly about infancy. He had no children. He was, with his twin Sabine, on the young end of the eight children in his family. While our default image of Bonhoeffer is of a deadly serious young man, he had a playful side, enjoying games and parties. His nieces and nephews adored him.

But his theology of the Incarnation, his wisdom about God as the Christ Child, didn't grow out of his personal affection for little ones he'd known or cradled. He simply read Scripture carefully, understanding God's paradoxical wisdom. God showed us God in the birth of a child, "not the revolutionary deed of a strongman, or the breathtaking discovery of a sage, or the pious deed of a saint." We look here and there for hope, meaning, security, or just what to do next. Bonhoeffer understands that there is only one place to go for help, for hope, for salvation. And that "one" is our next big theological word in our threefold highlight of Bonhoeffer's understanding of God and Scripture.

Deuteronomy 6:4-9: The Lord Our God Is One

What could be more self-evident than that God is one, that there is one God and only one God? Jews recite the Shema, "The Lord our God is one," and Christians profess "I believe in one God...in one Lord Jesus Christ." And yet, we broken, fallen human beings have this nagging tendency to bow down and worship deities that are fakes, multiples of one. Like those Israelites forging the golden calf, we lunge for something more immediate, more tangible, for what might stuff our pocketbooks or what suits our personal preferences. Whatever you give your heart to, whatever you think will make or break you, whatever you're certain will deliver the good life: this is your god. And we don't just sub one in for the real One. The human heart is, as John Calvin put it, "a perpetual factory of idols."[10] Grab a handful. Cover your bases.

For years as a pastor, I would name money or pleasure or "me" or even our nation as the god of choice, these idols that hook us so easily. More recently, I've come to see that the reigning idol in our day is political ideology. We truly believe that if our party, our candidate, our angle on what's good for America wins, all will be well and the kingdom will dawn. And if we lose, the apocalypse might just crush us all. When a candidate takes on the aura of absolute authority, Christians should be very wary. C. S. Lewis famously said, "I am a democrat [that is, a proponent of democracy] because I believe in the Fall of Man....Mankind is so fallen that no man can be trusted with unchecked power over his fellows."[11]

What Bonhoeffer witnessed, and what horrified him, was the gleeful kowtowing to Hitler, the mindless masses asking no questions about his gradual seizure of total power. Bonhoeffer, in fact, was the first, or nearly the first, to call out the idolatry and the sheer danger of this cult. In 1933, only two days after Hitler had seized power, Bonhoeffer broadcast an address on public radio. His pointed criticism was of "the Führer Principle," the idea that one great leader at the top could literally embody all the German people, and thus, on his own dictate policy, the economy, war, and even who lives and who dies.

Bonhoeffer explained how his German listeners were being manipulated by Hitler, who played on their humiliation in the wake of losing World War I and the miseries of the economy, casting himself as the great savior and redeemer, while denouncing all his enemies as godless. Just as Bonhoeffer was warning listeners about turning any leader into an idol, making the Führer (the German word for "leader") into a "mis-leader," somewhere in the middle of his clinching sentence, "Leaders who set themselves up as gods mock God," the microphone was abruptly shut off.[12]

It's not clear whether the Nazis cut him off or he'd just run over his time. But there can be little doubt that he was fast becoming someone the Nazis would want dead. We are shocked, and yet grateful, that he somehow survived twelve more years! Repeatedly, in sermons, speeches, and writings, he clarified that we, as Christians, have just one Führer. His approach echoed something vital in the New Testament we skate right past, not knowing the context: When Scripture says "Christ is Lord," those who first heard it were oppressed by a Roman culture where everyone had to swear "Caesar is Lord." "Christ is Lord" clearly implied "and Caesar isn't."

Subversive. Treasonous. To say it out loud was to invite persecution and death.

This was the year, 1933, that Bonhoeffer was working as a professor at the University of Berlin, lecturing on "Christology: Who is Jesus Christ?" His razor-sharp thoughts, fixed on a profound reading of Scripture, can help us, even today, understand how what we truly believe about Jesus defines our worldview—and how we too often let our preferred worldview twist what we should believe about Jesus into something perverse.

Christ enters our world of sin and death "in such a way as to hide in it in weakness. . . . He goes incognito as a beggar among beggars, as an outcast among the outcast."[13] Indeed, we only have Christ as the crucified and humiliated one. So profound, so biblical, so at odds with the Nazi-loving mobs, and so full of empathy for the embattled poor, and for the Jews, and for a world falling apart.

Exodus 20:3-5: No Other God

Other pastors and theologians shuddered as well. In late May of 1934, 139 of them gathered in Barmen-Wuppertal to strategize.[14] How should the church respond? Their reply to Hitler was not political, nor was it military. Theology—good theology, a faithful understanding of God—was at stake. Dogged fans of Hitler were running roughshod over good, faithful reading of the Bible. So these pastors laid the groundwork for what would be known as the Confessing Church, the minority who dared to be, not radical, but faithful. And that's where the word *one* was key.

Shocked by the extremism of so many Christians in Germany, they unanimously approved the Barmen Theological Declaration, a surprisingly simple document of obvious stuff, citing Scripture, clearly contradicting the mindless fawning of Christians over Hitler. Largely written by Bonhoeffer's mentor, Karl Barth, this declaration consisted of six simple theses, each one a Bible citation followed by a short affirmative theological statement, and then an added condemnation of the distortions being fallen for. The problem, these wise theologians understood, was heresy, not just bad politics. Always, in every age, faithful theology will speak the desperately needed truth into any and all political and social trouble.

The first thesis of Barmen stated:

> Jesus Christ, as he is attested to us in Holy Scripture, is the one Word of God whom we have to hear, and whom we have to trust and obey in life and in death. We reject the false doctrine that the church could and should recognize as a source of its proclamation, beyond and besides this one Word of God, yet other events, powers, historic figures, and truths as God's revelation.[15]

Anything radical here? Only if you've been hypnotized by a political ideology out of whack with Scripture. Basic Christian stuff: Christ is Lord, the only Lord. No impostors for us.

Barmen's words infuriated the Nazis, who weren't even mentioned! Simple, scriptural truth spoke loudly and clearly in straightforward judgment of what was going on. Opposition to Hitler wasn't political preference; it was all about Scripture. Mere words, but with a very different kind of power.

We, too, might ponder what it would look like for our viewpoints on politics, voting, and citizenship to be driven by our reading of

Scripture and not just a handpicked verse here or there or what somebody else told us is biblical. We might just have to discard much of what we've trusted and what we were sure was spot on and shift to a new script, one we'd never dreamed we'd get attached to. And not just the opposite party! Something higher than both the well-meaning but terribly flawed options thrust upon us in our political world.

Bonhoeffer didn't denounce such idol worship without severe consequences. He was hounded, threatened, and harassed. Probably the fact that he came from a fine, respected family provided him a little more cushion than other pastors. But in 1938, he was banned from the city of Berlin, his home. On a rainy night, Bonhoeffer and his best friend, Bethge, drove to Erfurt, the very city to which Martin Luther had fled when he was being pursued by both church and state for his courageous "Here I Stand" refusal to knuckle under after being told to hush. They found buildings, homes, and even churches draped in Nazi banners. The Wartburg Castle, where Luther hid out and translated the Bible into German, no longer had a cross at its entrance but a swastika, lit up at night by a floodlight.

Matthew 16:21-25: Christ Must Suffer

And then, after *Child* and *One*, we come to our third keyword: *Suffering.* Bonhoeffer's most compelling opening up of this idea of a "suffering God" is found in *The Cost of Discipleship.* In Matthew 16, Jesus asks the disciples what they've heard about him and then reveals that he will suffer and be rejected. Peter recoils at the very idea! And

Jesus upbraids him with a seemingly harsh "Get behind me, Satan" (Matthew 16:23).

Bonhoeffer doesn't leave this moment in the museum of religious artifacts from the past. This is happening now. Reflecting on Matthew 16, he notices that it is Peter, the Rock of the church, who sins here, moments after he has confessed Jesus as the Messiah, showing clearly that a suffering Messiah is not the kind of Lord the church wants. And it's personal: "Peter's protest displays his own unwillingness to suffer, and that means that Satan has gained entry into the Church, and is trying to tear it away from the cross of its Lord."[16]

Of course, as we will see in chapter 4, our aversion to the suffering Christ grows out of our suspicion that this suffering Christ might just bring us along into suffering with and for him! In 1940, Bonhoeffer wrote about the meaning of Advent, which we make into a pretty season of decorations and carols. Theologian and biographer Charles Marsh summarizes Bonhoeffer's stunning message:

> Jesus, the Jew, born homeless in a manger, the son of God. . . . This is the message of Advent—that God comes among us, but as a stranger! What an outrage! What an insult! Germans do not want a stranger for a savior. They want a "vacation from life," "a wisp of magic asking nothing and promising everything . . . to be transported into a fairy land."[17]

If you believe God is the heavenly provider of comfort and protection, or if you see Jesus as the sweet shepherd who gently guides us safely from the troubles of the world, or if you can fall for a muscular Jesus ferociously trouncing his foes, you have not spent time beneath the cross of Jesus or surveying the wondrous cross. God thought, I want them to know my heart and to love me. So God became human like the rest of us, a vulnerable, weak infant in his mother's womb, and then God bore the shame and utter agony of death on the cross.

The centurion was right: "Truly this man was the Son of God" (Mark 15:39)—not some other man or any other man. This is the good news and our hope: If you suffer, when you suffer, if and when you feel forsaken by God, even in your dying, you are not distant from God at all. You could not be closer or more loved and enveloped in mercy and hope. As Bonhoeffer said repeatedly, "Only the suffering God can help."[18]

It's ultimately about love. In chapter 1, we looked closely at Bonhoeffer's great sermons on 1 Corinthians 13, a text that concludes with "the greatest of these [among faith, hope, and love] is love" (1 Corinthians 13:13). Bonhoeffer is eloquent here and casts a lovely light on suffering: "Faith and hope enter into eternity transformed into the shape of love. In the end everything must become love. Perfection's name is love. But the sign of perfect love in this world bears the name cross."[19]

Bonhoeffer reminds us that in the cross we see Jesus turning out to be "the opposite of everything a religious person expects from God."[20] We might wish to say that God is in control or that God is omnipotent. But what greater argument could there be that God is not omnipotent? Or perhaps rather that God chooses not to function omnipotently?

Jürgen Moltmann, another student of Karl Barth's, points out that God isn't the God of all those definitions and long fancy terms like "omniscient," "infinite," or "omnipotent." The God of Scripture is all love, and love never controls. "A God who is only omnipotent is in himself an incomplete being, for he cannot experience helplessness and powerlessness. Omnipotence can indeed be longed for and worshipped by helpless men, but omnipotence is never loved; it is only feared."[21] I wonder whether Moltmann was reflecting on his teenage years in Germany under the terror of Hitler. He certainly was a careful reader of Scripture, as was Bonhoeffer. The God of love suffers with and for us. This is simply the plain reality of Scripture.

Pressing further, Bonhoeffer helps us understand why so many of our most urgent prayers go unanswered. God simply isn't a machine with buttons or a genie in a bottle, ready to do our bidding. I know pious people who "claim" to have received answers to their prayers. But how many Germans prayed for shelter during the horrors of the war? How many Jews prayed to be liberated from the camps? How many mothers of soldiers on all sides prayed for their sons' safe return? God is with us in our suffering. God hears. God loves. Love "bears all things" (1 Corinthians 13:7).

If God lets God's self be pushed out of the world onto the cross, we needn't be nervous when we hear or read critics mocking Christ or simply saying, "There can't be a God." Scoffers ridicule believers, pointing to the mess the world is in or the tragic deaths of good people, and we can nod, for it was the mess of the world that Jesus entered to love and that caused his tragic death.

Paul admits constantly that this suffering of God in Christ is an intellectual scandal. Stephen Hawking, the brilliant physicist, proved in his much-ballyhooed *The Theory of Everything* that we can explain all of reality without recourse to there being a god. Church members asked me to debunk Stephen Hawking! I could only reply that he was actually right: we don't *have* to believe; there is and should not be any airtight proof you couldn't reject for God. Love always risks rejection. Love can never make you love in return.

This clear understanding of the suffering God dawned on Bonhoeffer largely due to his careful reading of Scripture but also because of his life experiences, which he always viewed through the lens of Scripture. Bonhoeffer had grown up in a comfortable home, not wealthy but with sufficient resources to have a second home in the mountains, and the kids could study music and travel to other countries.

He learned about suffering over time. His brother Walter and two million other Germans were killed in World War I. Poverty spiked all over Germany in the months after the war. In his travels, Bonhoeffer noticed the poor and heavily burdened people, victims of injustice in Paris and then North Africa, and most pointedly in the United States. He arrived in New York not long after the stock market crash; he saw people standing in bread lines—and not just any people but his fellow worshippers at Abyssinian Baptist Church. He and his friend Jean Lassere took a long driving tour through the Jim Crow South, appalled by the conditions and treatment of impoverished African Americans in Alabama and Mississippi. When he read about a Black man being tortured and then hanged by a lynching mob, he reflected on the image of a "black Christ" being led out into a field by a "white Christ."[22]

In his first pastoral charge in Barcelona, he began to notice the poor, hungry, and homeless. Many had been caught in the crossfire between the repressions of the brutal dictator Primo de Rivera and armed revolts against his regime. Later, when assigned to pastor a small church in Berlin's poorest neighborhood, he spent countless hours with vulnerable and troubled kids and found hope and joy among them. All that he'd read in his theology books was finding its way more deeply into his heart—that the face of Christ was to be found not just in majestic glory but in the ordinary, downtrodden, broken people. Hadn't Jesus told us it would be so in Matthew 25? The more Bonhoeffer learned about human suffering, the more he understood Jesus Christ as co-sufferer.

2 Corinthians 12:9: Strength Made Perfect in Weakness

Paul's words, "My strength is made perfect in weakness" (2 Corinthians 12:9), rumbled around in Bonhoeffer's mind and heart for a long time after he visited a hospital in Bethel that cared for people with seizures and various mental and physical disabilities. Bonhoeffer had never encountered such challenged yet wonderful people. He wrote to his grandmother that being defenseless gives them deep insights into what life with God is like. He witnessed the image of God clearly visible among the weakest of people.

He also understood all too well that Hitler was ruthless in his determination to eliminate not just Jews but also the sick and the weak—all the vulnerable people. State-favored and state-favoring churches published a statement that is appalling, coming from pastors:

> In the fatal struggle for German freedom,...church leadership has shown itself to be too weak....We want our church to fight at the head of the decisive struggle for the existence or nonexistence of our people....We know something about Christian duty and love toward the helpless, but we also demand that our people be protected from the incapable and less worthy.[23]

Ah, that fatal word *but.* Bonhoeffer, in sharp contrast, preached a sermon to his London congregation on 2 Corinthians 12:9. He acknowledged that it is "human nature to keep away from all problems that might make us feel uncomfortable."[24] We deal with weakness every day, but deny it or strive to overcome it. Asking his congregation whether they had ever witnessed a greater mystery than "the poor, the insane, a cripple, a socially exploited person, a coloured person in a white country, an untouchable," he invited them (and invites us) to realize "you are inseparably bound together with such unfortunate people."

Yes, critics like Nietzsche and Hitler have always trashed Christianity for being a religion of the weak. But weakness is the truth in all of us, and so we see in the seemingly weak the humbling truth about ourselves. And how we approach them is how we approach Christ. "The Christian relation between the strong and the weak is that the strong has to look up to the weak and never to look down. Weakness is holy, therefore we devote ourselves to the weak." Indeed, "Christianity means a devaluation of all human values and the establishment of a new order of values in the sight of Christ."

So who was God to Bonhoeffer? Beginning in silence, his thoughts, passion, and resulting life commitment to God centered around those three key words: *Child. One. Suffering.* Nothing original to Bonhoeffer here! He had simply heard the Word.

3

GOD HAS SPOKEN TO US

When someone asks me to recommend a book on prayer, I almost always suggest Bonhoeffer's *Psalms: The Prayer Book of the Bible*. Yes, it's very short, simple, and accessible. And it's exceedingly profound and overflowing with wisdom. And, frankly, it's not exactly what folks are usually looking for. We crave some guidance in how to concentrate better or how to make our prayers more effective. Bonhoeffer shows zero interest in such matters and instead leads us into a very different space, a very biblical space of prayer.

Luke 11:1: Lord, Teach Us to Pray

He begins *Psalms* with that moment when the disciples ask Jesus, "Lord, teach us to pray." Clearly, they saw something remarkable, even incandescent, about Jesus's praying, and they wanted in on it. For us, the idea of needing to be taught to pray may be surprising. Don't you just pray? As in whatever is on your heart? Or whatever you need or long for? Bonhoeffer names "a dangerous error, surely very widespread among Christians, to think that the heart can pray by itself. For them we confuse wishes, hopes, sighs, laments, rejoicings—all of which the heart can do by itself—with prayer."[1] Okay, I thought that's what prayer was. So what else might it be?

"Prayer does not mean simply to pour out one's heart. It means rather to find the way to God and to speak with him, whether the heart is full or empty." Indeed, "God is not determined by our moods. Do not wait until being overtaken by feeling to encounter God. Prayer must be practiced."[2] So it's not a mood or feeling, and it's not a batch of requests, but a practice.

How then might we speak with God? With sheer genius, especially given that Bonhoeffer wasn't a parent and didn't spend a lot of time with very young children, he draws the perfect analogy—of how a child learns to talk. A child doesn't just start talking. Parents speak to the child, and the child learns the speech of the parents. So we learn to speak with God because God has spoken to us—and speaks to us.

How? In the Psalms, Bonhoeffer read and prayed psalms daily and encouraged others to do the same. His *why* is intriguing. A psalm may or may not give voice to what is in my heart in the moment, which is a gift: "If we are to pray aright, perhaps it is quite necessary that we pray contrary to our own heart. Not what we want to pray is important, but what God wants us to pray."[3] On our own, we would only ask God for what we want God to do for us. "But God wants it otherwise. The richness of the Word of God ought to determine our prayer, not the poverty of our heart."

For Bonhoeffer, therefore, prayer is more silence than talking. Very early in *Life Together*, thinking about our shared life with God, he indulges in a little list of texts advocating silence, but his favorite seems to be Psalm 65:2: "Praise befits you in silence, O God." (I'd have chosen Psalm 62:1: "For God alone my soul waits in silence; / from him comes my salvation.") His insight on opening the day in quiet? "We are silent early in the morning because God should have the first word, and we are silent before going to bed because the last word also belongs to God."[4] There's the frame, the bracketing, the arms of holy embrace for my day and my night.

His morning devotions then moved to either a silent or unison reading of the Psalms. We can't ignore how Bonhoeffer shows us that what had been normal forever in Christianity struck people in his day (as in ours) as controversial or radical. The Psalms have always been at the heart of Christian prayer. But in the toxic air of Nazi Germany, lifting up any Old Testament book as even worthy of attention seemed radical. Nazi officials frowned on anyone publishing positive words about any Jewish book and insisted that they desist. Bonhoeffer did not desist, and so we honor him, along with Jews and Christians through history, by pondering the Psalms. And we become one with Jesus, as the Psalms Bonhoeffer loved were the prayers Jesus loved and prayed.

Psalm 119: The Word Penetrating and Dwelling in Us

For Bonhoeffer, the richness of the Word of God determined far more than just his praying. If our project here together is to read the

Bible with Bonhoeffer, or even to dare to read the Bible like Bonhoeffer, we might benefit from stepping back and looking at what he thought about the Bible, how he approached it, and what he expected from it. He wasn't obsessed with questions such as, Is the Bible literally or factually accurate? or even, Is the Bible inspired? He seems from an early age to have found himself deeply immersed in Scripture and ready to engage enthusiastically in its contents.

Let me allow Bonhoeffer to speak for himself and to us about what to expect from Scripture and how to dig into the text. In a letter to a friend, he wrote, "The heart of God opens itself to us in God's Word."[5] I love this: friends talking with each other about God's heart and Word! Reflecting on his favorite psalm, Psalm 119 (not many people's favorite!), he notes, "It is never enough to have read God's word. It must enter us deeply, dwell in us like the Holiest of Holies in the sanctuary."[6] Attentive to the literal text of verse 6, "having my eyes fixed on all your commandments," he specifically riffs on "eyes fixed" and "all":

> I look at God's commandments when I base my decisions neither on other people nor even on my own thoughts or experiences, but rather when I ask ever anew, even if contrary to my pious thoughts and experiences, for what God commands me. I can be put to shame even by my most pious decisions and ways but never by God's commandment.

This must be maturity in prayer, going with what is contrary to my most devout thoughts!

And then, in a letter to his brother-in-law Rüdiger, he writes, "This is how I read the Bible now. I ask of each passage: What is God saying to us here? And I ask God that he would help us hear what he wants to say. So, we no longer look for general, eternal truths," which he suggests are "somehow self-evident to us. Instead, we seek the will of God, who is altogether strange to us, whose ways are not our ways and whose thoughts are not our thoughts."[7]

Then he added: "Since I learned to read the Bible this way—which has not been long at all—it becomes more wonderful to me with each day."[8] I love this idea of family members talking about what God is saying and that, with Scripture, we are especially on the lookout for what is strange, for what collides with our pet ideas about life and God.

Bonhoeffer taught his seminary students that

> Brief verses cannot and should not take the place of reading the Scripture as a whole. . . . Holy Scripture does not consist of individual passages; it is a unit and is intended to be used as such. As a whole the Scriptures are God's revealing Word. Only in the infiniteness of its inner relationships, in the connection of Old and New Testaments, of promise and fulfillment, sacrifice and law, law and gospel, cross and resurrection, faith and obedience, having and hoping, will the full witness to Jesus Christ the Lord be perceived.[9]

Bonhoeffer reminds me in a way of St. Francis of Assisi. I've said and written many times that Francis took the Bible literally, not fretting over issues like historical accuracy or theological authority, but as in whatever he found there literally became his to-do list for the day. He read. He didn't come up with any clever spin on it. He didn't weaponize it to judge others. This towering intellectual read Scripture, probed its words and the spaces between them relentlessly, and kept listening for a Word, not one that would prop up his preferences or make his life cozier, but for one that was clear, timely, and hugely important. And then it made its way onto his to-do list, which fundamentally altered the whole direction of his life.

Jeremiah 20:7: No Good Trying to Resist

Reading Bonhoeffer, we are challenged not to hunt for some Scripture to soothe or perk up our lives as they are. Scripture becomes the roadmap, our marching orders, the corrective lenses through which we make sense of our lives. In October 1933, Bonhoeffer had left his increasingly troubled homeland by moving to London, where he pastored two small churches of German expatriates. But he kept hearing about the tumult back home and was harshly rebuked by his theological mentor Karl Barth, who'd not been asked for counsel and only learned Bonhoeffer's whereabouts after the fact: "Get back to your post in Berlin straightaway!... You need to be here with all guns blazing!... Your church's house is on fire!"[10]

Barth wasn't the only one angered by Bonhoeffer. As he was leaving Germany, Nazi authorities sternly warned him not to speak against them while in England. His first winter there, he preached on the prophet Jeremiah, sounding as if he were talking to himself, as if Jeremiah's life was held up as a mirror of his own. Jerusalem had corrupted itself, so God's prophet was suffering intense turmoil and peril, repeatedly expressing how he wished he'd never been called. But there was nothing he could do. Bonhoeffer was no more eager than Jeremiah to be a prophet. But his resistance was futile. He sensed in Jeremiah's story his own: "As he was running away, he was seized by the word, by the call."[11]

Before you read further, think of what God might be asking of you and of God's church today. Bonhoeffer explained that this call is far from the longing in your heart. God's call comes from outside you. It's not what we want to do, or even what we want to do for God, but what God wants us to do. But aren't we free? Bonhoeffer speaks tenderly yet firmly to his people and to himself, and also to us: "It is no good trying to resist." Yet if we hear and then go, no matter how stony the road, "this foreign, this faraway, unfamiliar, overwhelming word becomes the incredibly familiar, incredibly near, persuading, captivating, enticing word of the Lord's love, yearning for his creature." Lovely.

As we listen in on Bonhoeffer's wrestling with hearing and following God's Word, we discover an echo of what it means for us to do the same. Bonhoeffer compares God's call to a lasso thrown over your head. The world will see you, like Jeremiah, as a fool, "but a fool who is extremely dangerous to people's peace and comfort." Immediately after this sermon, Theodor Heckel, one of those vile bishops who wound up *Heil*-ing Hitler, paid Bonhoeffer a personal visit in London and suggested he hush.

But Bonhoeffer could not hush. Still unpacking Jeremiah in the sermon, he spoke, not just to his people or even to himself, but to God: "It was you who started this with me. It was you who pursued me and would not let me go.... God, you enticed me [taking up Jeremiah 20:7 literally as his own prayer!].... I cannot get away from you anymore; you have carried me off as your booty." He then reminds those Londoners of the pastors and people back in Germany who, with valor, were even then risking life and limb to name the lies of the Nazis. I wonder if anyone stomped out in rage on hearing this sermon. Bonhoeffer could not have been truer to the heart of Scripture.

Even with his razor-sharp intellect and not one but two doctorates in theology, Bonhoeffer always had this lovely, uncomplicated trust in Scripture. In his first pastoral work, he was tasked with the teenagers in the little Lutheran church in Barcelona. Then, when back in Berlin, he was pastor to the poorest and most poorly behaved adolescents in the whole city. Bonhoeffer had no clue what to do with kids; he'd grown up in a cultured, well-behaved family. At first, he tried to deploy logic and philosophical thoughts on the youth assigned to him, which got him nowhere. So he resorted to telling, quite straightforwardly, the stories from the Bible and found his teens to be attentive, even enthralled. He discovered he didn't need to dress up the Bible to make it relevant. It simply *was* relevant and very true to life and revealing of what life with God could be like. That church, the Zion Church (Zionskirche), still takes pride in his season there, with an impressionistic bronze statue of him in the churchyard.

Matthew 5–7: I Discovered the Bible

Perhaps the most puzzling and then terribly hopeful words Bonhoeffer ever wrote were those written in 1936 after he'd been a pastor, teacher, and theologian for many years, reflecting on a stunning change that gradually came over him:

> I threw myself into my work in an extremely un-Christian and not at all humble fashion. . . . I was terribly alone. . . . But then something different came, something that has changed and transformed my life

> to this very day. For the first time, I discovered the Bible.... That too, is an awful thing to say. I had often preached, I had seen a great deal of the church, had spoken and written about it—and yet I was not yet a Christian but rather in an utterly wild and uncontrolled fashion my own master. I do know that at the time I turned the cause of Jesus Christ into an advantage for myself.... The Bible, especially the Sermon on the Mount, freed me from all this.[12]

How many great Christians have undergone this very startling transformation? Luther, Wesley, St. Francis? Bonhoeffer knew his Bible well. But he'd missed it—perhaps because he was looking to it for "advantage for myself." For me, Bonhoeffer is one of a handful of friends among the communion of the saints who lovingly walk with me into a regular rediscovery of the Bible I've known, which must be what Bible study is finally all about.

His mentor, Karl Barth, reported on his own discovery of the book of Romans and what might just unfold for us when we are confronted by Scripture. For him, it's applying "creative energy" and "intuitive certainty," so that we "re-think the whole material and wrestle with it," until the walls that separate our day from the Bible's crumble and become transparent.[13] When this happens, there is a profound "conversation between the original record and the reader... until the distinction between yesterday and to-day becomes impossible." Indeed, "Paul knows of God what most of us do not know; and his Epistles enable us to know what he knew."

In this mode of engagement with the Bible, God speaks, and we listen—not to ourselves but to God. In *Creation and Fall*, Bonhoeffer ingenuously invites us to rethink one of our naive assumptions about the moral life. What does he call Adam hiding from God in the garden? Conscience! Thinking we know right from wrong, we are, in reality, in flight from God, but the idea that we have a conscience enables us to feel quite secure. "Conscience is not the voice of God in sinful man, but rather it is precisely the defense against that voice."[14] Resorting to relying on conscience is yet one more way we justify ourselves and do as we wish instead of being justified by God and doing what God asks. For Bonhoeffer, especially this newly awakened Bonhoeffer, Bible reading isn't collecting information or seeking affirmation. It is "self-relinquishment," "ready submission and active compliance."[15]

Genesis 3:1—Did God Really Say . . . ?

What stands out about Bonhoeffer's way of reading Scripture is his refusal to finesse things. We typically find ways to sidestep the most challenging passages, putting a reasonable spin on things. Jesus says, "Do not lay up treasure on earth" (Matthew 6:19), but we understandably have our savings and pension funds. We may recall Jesus says that if you give a dinner party, don't invite those who can invite you in return, but invite the poor, maimed, lame, and blind who cannot repay you (Luke 14:12-14), and so we drop off a bag of canned goods at church on our way to meet other good church friends for dinner, and feel we've fulfilled the spirit of what Jesus must have wanted.

A weekly Bible study group in my parish committed to hosting a dozen homeless guests for dinner once a month and decided it would be fun to invite them to join their Bible study and discuss whatever text had been covered the week before. On their first go-round, they'd explored "Sell all you have and give to the poor" (Mark 10:21). They handled it deftly with clever evasions, like "Jesus only meant for us to be willing to do this," or "I've got to provide for my family," or "Civilization would collapse if we all did this," and even "The poor wouldn't know how to handle so much money." Seven days later, after the text was read aloud, my Bible study people mostly stared down at their hands, unable to repeat that they should only be willing or that the poor would be clueless.

As a twenty-year-old professor in Berlin, Bonhoeffer probed the serpent's question to Adam and Eve: "Did God say 'You shall not eat of any tree of the garden'?" (Genesis 3:1), which he counts as "the first religious question in the world"[16]—chronologically first but also first in importance. We deploy this question all the time, asking things like, Did God really say this to me? Perhaps it does not apply in my particular case? Bonhoeffer perceives this as "the question that appears innocuous, but through it evil wins power in us, through it we become disobedient to God." What's the problem with this question? "It is that the false answer is contained within it. . . . Man is expected to be judge of God's word instead of simply hearing and doing it." You can't unsee that. We set ourselves up as judges of what's in God's word instead of hearing and doing.

Bonhoeffer reiterated this approach, powerfully, when he spoke at an ecumenical peace conference in Denmark in 1934. Germany had just left the League of Nations and was arming for war, to the vengeful delight of most Germans. With piercing sarcasm, Bonhoeffer addressed the way religious leaders were explaining away

Jesus's clear call for us to be peacemakers and to love our enemies—a commandment, not a slogan or a meme or a song:

> Has God not understood human nature well enough to know that wars must occur in this world, like laws of nature? Must God not have meant that we should talk about peace, to be sure, but that is not to be literally translated into action? Must God not really have said that we should work for peace, of course, but also make ready tanks and poison gas for security?

And then perhaps the most serious question:

> Did God say you should not protect your own people? Did God say you should leave your own a prey to the enemy? No, God did not say all that. What He has said is that there shall be peace among men—that we shall obey Him without further question, that is what He means. He who questions the commandment of God before obeying has already denied Him.[17]

We tremble a little just reading such strong, plain words.

Simple and Paradoxical Obedience

Bonhoeffer was no fool; he fully grasped the complexities and compromises of living as a Christian in this fallen world. So he gifts us with a much-needed distinction between "simple obedience" and "paradoxical obedience." Simple obedience is simply doing what the command asks. Paradoxical obedience accounts for the realities of the world. You have God-given responsibilities—for example, as a parent or a spouse—that compel you to what can seem to be disobedience to God's other simple commands. His example is "Do not lay up treasure on earth." Simple obedience would be refusing to save for retirement or your kid's college education, whereas paradoxical obedience leaves room for a bank account. Bonhoeffer had a bank account himself, of course.

But he was adamant that we can't let paradoxical obedience blind us to the radical commitment God asks from us. If all our obedience is paradoxical, we never respond to Christ's call to follow and we remain lords of our own lives. Bonhoeffer even suggests that only after we've engaged in simple obedience are we in a place to engage faithfully in paradoxical obedience. If we default to paradoxical obedience—that is, getting fancy with God's commands by fulfilling them in a way that is convenient for us—then we veer into what Bonhoeffer calls "cheap grace," which will be our central theme in chapter 4.

Clearly, God confronts people throughout Scripture with extraordinarily difficult choices. Bonhoeffer would warn us against the sneaky temptation of being "realistic." His Barcelona lecture early in his pastoral ministry about the dangers of the world and being prepared to fight and kill for your country, which he later regretted? He was just being "realistic." Or reasonable. I love Bonhoeffer's adamant remark to his brother Karl-Friedrich, who thought him a bit of a fanatic: "The day I become more 'reasonable,' I should have to chuck my whole theology."[18]

One haunting example Bonhoeffer reflects on is when God asked Abraham to sacrifice his long-awaited, beloved son, Isaac. Abraham defaulted to simple, not paradoxical, obedience, and raised the knife. When God stepped in at the last second, was Abraham just relieved?

Or was something more profound won because of his default to simple obedience? Bonhoeffer thought so:

> Abraham receives Isaac back, but henceforth he will have his son in quite a new way—through the Mediator and for the Mediator's sake. Since he had shown himself ready to obey God literally, he is now allowed to possess Isaac though he had him not—to possess him through Jesus Christ.[19]

Simple obedience isn't about a judgmental God double-daring you to follow the rules or else. It's about relationship—the deep, passionate kind. A young lover might sing, "I'd do anything for you, dear, anything." The zealous disciple, young or old, has what Maggie Ross called "a willingness for whatever."[20] In life, for Jesus's followers, it's not, What do I want to do? or even What do I want to do for God? but rather, What does God want me to do?

James 1:21-25: Doers of the Word

Sometimes we might envy the young when it comes to taking the Bible at face value and enacting what it says with abandon. The future seems wide open. No possibilities are foreclosed. After a few years, you've made some commitments, nothing risky for God per se, but not wicked, very fine and nice, actually. But you have a spouse or a mortgage or a career or some indebtedness, whatever entanglements that make it tough to do as those fishermen who became disciples, or Francis who became a saint, or Bonhoeffer who lost his life.

Yet there's something in being attentive to the young and their idealistic vision, their raw zeal to be real Christians that loosens things up a little for even the most entangled and frees us to be a little more of who we might have been and still might be. When Bonhoeffer was still in seminary, he wrote a remarkable sermon on James 1:21-25 that explicitly targeted young people ages sixteen to twenty. He was still in that age range himself!

But he also recognized his generation of young people had endured peculiar traumas in their short lives: the crushing losses from the pointless and grueling World War I. Tens of millions dead. The aftermath of hunger, economic devastation, and shame. James speaks of looking in a mirror, and Bonhoeffer invites all of us to see the faces of youth who've borne all this, very different from those who've grown up "in a bucolic landscape or *playing* war."[21] These youth bear "the marks of unrelenting severity"—a severity that searches for hope, purpose, freedom. That search raises the urgent question of God.

He also intuited they would be the ones to face more horrific troubles to come. It's only 1926. No Hitler—yet. But Bonhoeffer could already detect a darkening chaos descending. With remarkable foresight, Bonhoeffer warned against submission to any authority other than God, alerting them to the ways we make political strong men into idols. James speaks of freedom, which we Americans presume means we can choose our own path, as did so many Germans then. Attentive to James's directive to "welcome the implanted word" (James 1:21), Bonhoeffer pushes aside the vain notion that any and all paths might be valid. The only path that matters is the path from God to us.

Notice the order: not from us to God! In this, although Bonhoeffer had not yet met his theological hero Karl Barth, he was joining the vanguard of young theologians who were reversing years of religious thinking that began with human needs, questions, and wants and then moved to God for the answers—which probably sounds normal to us today. For Bonhoeffer, God being God comes first; ours is to answer. I'm moved by his appeal: "God has planted his word in the midst of our sordid existence. It lives there in silence, and for many it is completely hidden. God is already with us; indeed, God is truly already *in* us. Believe it! Accept it!" This is hope, not choosing whether to find God or figuring out how to find God. God finds us. God speaks to us.

Bonhoeffer notices that James invites us to meek obedience—but not just to any authority. Not to myself: "What is the meaning of obedience if I myself become God?" And not to any political authority: "Religion is submission to a clearly acknowledged authority. . . . Is there not a certain pride in being obedient to a powerful person?" What a profound, insightful question!

He riffs on James's reflection on looking into a mirror (wordplay intended). He'd seen, as have we all, churchgoers who show up at church and "hear the word," glance then into the mirror, and feel a certain pride, convincing themselves they've done enough. But have they really heard?

And not just heard: James urges his readers—and with Bonhoeffer's assistance, all of us—to be "not just hearers but doers of the word." This young seminarian clarifies that this Word isn't guidelines or rules we've figured out or find helpful, no matter how crucial they seem to us. No, the Word we hear and do is God's—from and for God. Be "doers of the Word" (James 1:22). Not "Be doers of what you like and enjoy," but of the Word. And we need to be vigilant never to paste a God label on something out of sync with Scripture: "Demonstrate that your belief in God is really a belief in *God*." Ponder that for a while.

The sermon is punctuated with repeated moments of insistence, as if Bonhoeffer worries people are napping or not taking all this seriously. "Think about it!" "Take it seriously!" "Decide!" And finally, to the generation that survived the ravages of World War I, who wanted safety and security above all else, Bonhoeffer concludes his sermon by crying out, "Come out, humanity, from the foxhole. Come out to where the breeze is blowing free, where the bullets whistle by." Did listeners holler *Amen!* and raise their hands to get out into that breeze?

John 8:32: The Most Revolutionary Text

For the moment, block from your mind the fact of Bonhoeffer's arrest and execution, even from the politics of Germany at that time, and weigh how Bonhoeffer thought about the Word of God simply as a pastor and a person. What an obviously high view of the Word he held—not bickering over its inerrancy but revering it and taking its words, especially its hardest words, as marching orders.

When Bonhoeffer was a pastor to students, he drafted a sermon for them on John 8:32, which he dubbed "the most revolutionary text in the New Testament."[22] Did he believe that, or was he piquing their interest? By 1932, he was yearning for some kind of revolution in the hearts of his fellow Germans, not based on political wisdom or economic benefits but solely on the Word of God.

He had recently been with his mentor Karl Barth in person for the first time, so it's no surprise we hear Bonhoeffer exposing once more our understandable but flawed habit of approaching the spiritual life from the wrong direction. "We have become accustomed to seeing religion as something that corresponds to a need of the human soul and satisfies this need." Seems obvious, right? I have needs. Surely God should satisfy them. But this thinking puts you and me at the center instead of God. And we may well be (and probably are) actually mistaken about what we truly need and what would satisfy.

Bonhoeffer reverses field: "We forget the one most important question," not "What do I need?" but "whether religion is also something true, whether it is the truth." Nothing matters but whether religion is true. And we recognize truth "not through free research, not through disinterested thinking and searching for it, but solely through the free attempt to base one's life for once completely on the word of Christ."

The political chatter around Berlin was all about Hitler restoring the freedom of the oppressed German people. Bonhoeffer dared to declare that "real truth is different from that slogan-like truth." Real truth redeems people and the world and sets us truly free for God. "It opens the person's eyes to the fact that up to now he had lived in lies, without freedom and in fear."

Should anyone listening miss Bonhoeffer's point or think he's speaking of somebody else in some other place and time, Bonhoeffer clarifies that freedom was being spoken of "in a way that the passions of a German are aroused and set everything in him aquiver, making him forget everything else." Like a wise therapist, he exposes what is hidden beneath the absurd embrace of evil as truth: "We are all afraid of the truth. And this fear is basically our fear of God. God is truth and no other. And we are afraid of him, afraid he will suddenly place us in the light of the truth and unmask us in our deceitfulness." Can't we see that "the political lie, the self-serving lie, have a devastating power over us."

And then Bonhoeffer takes us to the cross: "You hated God's truth about yourself. You crucified it, and you set up your own truth. . . . You lived as if you were alone in the world. You found in yourself the source of truth, which is only in God." Can you hear truth about yourself in his words? I know I can, and I am humbled and convicted.

Bonhoeffer then shifts, as Jesus did, from truth to being set free. Freedom isn't doing or thinking as I wish or prospering in this world. No, freedom is "becoming free from oneself, from the lie that I am the only one there, that I am the center of the world." As we will see in our next chapter, as deadly serious as following Christ turns out to be, it's not a heavier yoke but the one way to joy. God's commandments aren't restrictive but liberating. Human laws restrict. God's laws liberate and enliven.

Later, Bonhoeffer turned to truth's opposite and its vilest foe, stupidity, which is as dangerous an enemy of the good as evil itself. "One may wage protest against evil; evil can be exposed and, if need be, overcome by force. But stupidity mounts a broad and insidious defense."[23] With stupidity, "facts that contradict one's prejudgment simply need not be believed . . . and when facts are irrefutable they are just pushed aside as inconsequential."

He presses on:

> The fact that the stupid person is often stubborn must not blind us to the fact that he is not independent. In conversation with him, one virtually feels that one is dealing not at all with him as a person, but with slogans, catchwords and the like that have taken possession of him. He is under a spell, blinded, misused, and abused in his

> very being. Having thus become a mindless tool, the stupid person will also be capable of any evil and at the same time incapable of seeing that it is evil.

Political ideology in our day, we simply must confess, no matter how very informed and clever we believe we are in what we think, is just such stupidity. I often say that if you only hang around with people like you, you become arrogant and ignorant. The cure for ignorance, and for arrogance, is a refusal to be stupid, to get curious and be open to facts that contradict our prejudgments. The antidote for ignorance and arrogance is tucked inside John 8:32, which must be the most revolutionary text in Scripture: "You shall know the truth, and the truth shall set you free" (John 8:32).

Chapter 4

FOLLOW ME

If I could travel back in time and sit in on any class taught by anyone of my choosing, I might well choose to be in that little imperiled seminary at Finkenwalde during the winter of 1935–36 listening to Dietrich Bonhoeffer deliver his lectures that would wind up published as *The Cost of Discipleship*. I imagine myself bracing for the cold north winds blowing off the Baltic Sea, with only seven hours of daylight up there at 53° longitude. Another dozen students are there, inside but with precious little heat and dim lighting. But no worries. Professor Bonhoeffer, not yet thirty years old, strides in, shuffles his papers, and begins to speak of cheap grace and costly grace—and we're not chilly any longer. There's some fire in this young man, and his words burn into our minds and hearts.

An adjective that often attaches itself to Bonhoeffer's name is "radical." Even those who know him best tend to speak of his "radical" Christianity. I think he would sigh and shake his head over this. Bonhoeffer is "radical" only to the degree to which you have watered down Christianity. If you're part of a church or if you dig a spirituality that is all about your needs being met and your comforts assured or if your religion is about nice people doing nice things with other nice people in a nice place, then Bonhoeffer will blow your mind and might leave you a little concussed or confused. He will strike you as radical indeed.

But if you've read your Bible without reading into it what you hope to find and not skimming until you find the parts that support your preconceived notions—that is, if you've taken Christianity at face value, if you've taken Jesus's words as meaning what they say, then Bonhoeffer won't seem radical at all. He's simply Christian.

In this chapter, I want to walk you through Bonhoeffer's simplest reading of Scripture, which we find in his well-known book *The Cost of Discipleship*. I've always said that if you pick up this book and read just the first five or six pages, your fingers will get singed. You might notice some steam or smoke curling upward. Bonhoeffer was simply on fire. But he wouldn't agree with me: The fire wasn't his. It was Jesus who was on fire. And Jesus might just ignite a fire in you, or in your church, by way of Bonhoeffer.

So those pages that singe your fingers? Buckle up. Hold your breath. With Germans who'd staked their religious lives on grace, the free grace taught so eloquently by their own German Martin Luther in mind, Bonhoeffer explodes onto the page:

> Cheap grace is the deadly enemy of our Church. We are fighting to-day for costly grace. Cheap grace means grace sold on the market like cheapjacks' wares. The sacraments, the forgiveness of sin, and the consolations of religion are thrown away at cut prices.... Grace without price; grace without cost...cheap covering for sins; no contrition is required, still less any real desire to be delivered from

> sin. . . . Instead of following Christ, let the Christian enjoy the consolations of his grace![1]

And that's just from his first two pages. Did any religious book ever get off to a hotter start? The rarities in my old, tattered copy of the book are the very few words and phrases that are *not* underlined or circled. The churches had clearly cheapened themselves, as had run-of-the-mill Christians. Readers today feel dizzy and terribly inadequate; they may slip into a bit of a spiritual funk on confronting Bonhoeffer's powerful words. But his tone isn't severe reprimand but rather a plaintive invitation and a promise that even though we do not know where this path will lead, "we do know that it will be a road of boundless mercy. Discipleship means joy." It's the treasure in the field.

Matthew 4:18-22: Follow Me!

As Bonhoeffer unpacks his thoughts on costly grace, he zeroes in on not just his but also Jesus's crucial word: *Follow*. Costly grace "is costly because it calls us to follow, and it is grace because it calls us to follow Jesus Christ." After all, grace was costly to God; it costs God the life of God's own Son. "What has cost God much cannot be cheap for us." He reminds us that a student is not above their master.

The bulk of his lectures focused on the Sermon on the Mount. But the first disciples got to that mount because Jesus had shown up on the shore of Galilee and invited people who didn't know him very well yet, "Follow me." Perhaps the greatest miracle in the New Testament is that they did just that. They dropped everything—livelihood, family, security—and traipsed off after him, with no strategy, no budget, no clue where they were going or how the journey would end.

My path into ministry—actually my path to being a serious Christian—took a dramatic turn one night in college. I'd dipped my toe into church, but I was guardedly watching, being entertained, keeping a safe distance. Friends were bugging me to join them in a Bible study, but I had no interest—until one night I had a vivid dream of Jesus (how did I recognize him?) standing by the sea and saying, "Follow me." Okay, I thought, I'll try the Bible study—once.

I showed up, anxious, expecting I'd be bored. But then the leader opened his Bible and said "Friends, tonight I want us to explore Matthew 4:19 where Jesus says to us, 'Follow me.'" Nowhere to run and hide. I could only begin my lifelong attempt to follow.

Bonhoeffer reminds his listeners, including us, that Jesus didn't say "Believe in me" or "Believe these things about me." Jesus didn't say "Nice to meet you, I'll be back next Sunday." No. "The call goes out, and without any further ado the obedient deed of the one called follows. The disciple's answer is not a spoken confession of faith in Jesus. Instead, it is the obedient deed."[2] Bonhoeffer acknowledges that this statement is "quite offensive to natural reason," which seeks explanations or some time.

Bonhoeffer fast-forwards to those in Luke 9:57-62 who dream of following but have their quite plausible reasons for waiting. "Let me first. . . ." (see Luke 9:59, 61).[3] Such a person "wants to follow, but feels obliged to insist on his own terms," which reminds me of something I repeat often in preaching: "It's not what you want to do, or even what you want to do for God; it's what God wants you to do."

Bonhoeffer could speak for himself on the impact of the gospel that had converted him from thinking of Jesus and religion as "something of personal advantage for myself."

The book, which, by God's grace, survived Nazi censors and is still a bestseller today, was simply titled by Bonhoeffer as *Nachfolge*, the German word for "discipleship" or "following." It's profound in a way that the first English edition added "The Cost of" before the word *Discipleship*, as that title alone jars us out of our spiritual slumbers and reminds us of what is at stake. But what was lost? *Nachfolge* is actually an imperative. "Follow!" Jesus didn't leave things at "Think about me" or "Study about me." Jesus said, "*Follow me.*"

And Jesus said quite a few other things. Bonhoeffer is a literalist when it comes to what got printed in red letters in those old-school Bibles. Jesus wasn't kidding or speaking allegorically. When he said, "Follow me," "Love your enemy," and "Do not kill," he meant just that. To emphasize his strategy—or what he was simply passing along, Jesus's strategy—Bonhoeffer thumbs forward in Matthew to chapter 19, the familiar story of the rich young ruler.

Matthew 19:16-30: The Rich Young Ruler

Bonhoeffer is amused, as we all may be, by the young man's claim that he has always kept all the commandments. He'd probably not heard Jesus say anger is killing and lust is adultery! But being rich, he'd surely done some coveting. At any rate, his piety has been more about avoidance than doing; he's the prime example of Bonhoeffer's constant insistence that we think we are good by keeping our hands clean when God wills that we get our hands dirty doing for God and others. Those who neither steal nor murder "must close their eyes and ears to the injustice around them. Only at the cost of self-deception can they keep their private blamelessness clean from the stains of responsible action in the world."[4]

This rich man, like so many Jesus encountered, wanted to debate the true meaning of the commandments. Of course, if a commandment is at all ambiguous, you're absolved of responsibility for keeping it, right? And then we have clever ways of avoiding simple obedience. Bonhoeffer imagines the rich ruler's thought process: "In spite of Jesus' word, I want to remain rich, but I will become inwardly free from my riches and comfort my inadequacy with the forgiveness of sins and be in communion with Jesus by faith."[5] Ouch!

Then, with laugh-out-loud, biting sarcasm, Bonhoeffer offers a clear analogy:

> Anywhere else in the world where commands are given, the situation is clear. A father says to his child: go to bed! The child knows exactly what to do. But a child drilled in pseudotheology would have to argue thus: Father says go to bed. He means you are tired; he does not want me to be tired. But I can also overcome my tiredness by going to play. So, although father says go to bed, what he really means is go play.

As you may recall, in chapter 3, we spoke of Bonhoeffer's distinction between simple and paradoxical obedience. This young man is a wizard at the paradoxical! But Jesus asks something simple. And when simple obedience is rejected, we are into cheap grace.

We too have been trained—at church no less—to be wizards of the paradoxical. In chapter 3 I recounted the funny but telling episode of the Bible study group in my church deftly handling Jesus's words to sell all and give to the poor. Such finesse! Surely Jesus intended that command for this or that particular guy, not the rest of us. Jesus understands I've got to provide for my family; Western civilization would collapse if we followed that command; the poor wouldn't know how to handle that much money; Jesus only meant for me to be *willing* to sell all . . . blah blah blah. But after the Bible study members met with the homeless, shared a meal with them, grew to like them tremendously, they felt uncomfortable after reading the same text, after which there were crickets, uneasy glances, heads hung down, throats cleared.

Where and with whom we read the Bible matters. And when. Bonhoeffer read the Sermon on the Mount in his comfortable home growing up. But then he heard new resonances when he read it with African Americans in the Abyssinian Baptist Church, and then even more with seminarians hounded by the Gestapo. We, who join Bible study groups or do the work individually, might seek out new places and some different company for our times of reflection and growth. And we can open our hearts and minds to what people under duress, like Bonhoeffer, have to say to us.

We saw in chapter 3 how Bonhoeffer parsed that tense moment when Peter had just identified Jesus correctly as the Christ—as most Germans would have in the 1930s. What Peter won't tolerate is the suggestion that Jesus will suffer, which Bonhoeffer rightly diagnoses as Peter's own "aversion to submit himself to suffering. That is a way for Satan to enter the church."

When we shy away from sacrifice, from suffering in following Christ, could it be that the resulting gap between us and Jesus is the opening for Satan? Jesus must have caught Peter off guard by saying, "Get behind me, Satan" (Matthew 16:23). Bonhoeffer suggests Satan is back at it, hijacking the church and taking it far from the cross. Peter, as we know, would deny Christ three times when danger and evil were about to pounce. In that moment, Peter did not or could not understand the hard reality of what might be Bonhoeffer's most famous articulation of what Jesus was asking: "When Christ calls a man he bids him come and die" (as the original translation by R. H. Fuller phrased it). The original German literally means, "Every call of Christ leads into death."[6]

Matthew 5:1: The Sermon on the Mount

As I picture myself sitting at Bonhoeffer's feet in Finkenwalde, I might be a little dizzy from the way he's shaken me thus far. Now it's another day back in class, and finally he gets to the advertised subject matter: the Sermon on the Mount. I love the way Bonhoeffer reads slowly enough to show us what we miss when we skim ahead quickly. Matthew 5 doesn't begin with "Blessed are the poor in spirit," but rather "Seeing the crowds, he went up on the mountain, and when he sat down his disciples came to him."

Picture all that. Jesus sees the crowds. The crowds obviously see him. Then the disciples move but evidently not the crowd:

> The disciples—not so long before, they themselves were fully part of the crowd. They were just like all the others. Then Jesus' call came. So they left everything behind and followed him. Since then, they have belonged to Jesus—completely. Now they go with him,

> live with him, follow him wherever he leads them. Something has happened to them that has not happened to the others. This is an extremely unsettling and offensive fact, which is visibly evident to the crowd.[7]

You can't unsee that. Many see and hear Jesus. Only a few come to him and stick close. The rest of Jesus's sermon, and the rest of his ministry, is inviting the crowd that sees and hears no longer to remain part of the crowd, like everyone else, but to belong to him. Something might just happen to them. The disciples, and anyone else who would join them, are pronounced "blessed." We get confused about blessings, presuming blessings are comforts, pleasant things we crave. But the text reveals that the blessedness is simply following Jesus, who, after all, is the one who most exemplifies being poor in spirit, meek, merciful, pure in heart, and persecuted for righteousness. Answering his call actually has caused the disciples to be poor, tempted, and hungry!

How far is all this from some of the silly readings we've been fed? Robert Schuller twisted the Beatitudes (Matthew 5:1-12) into *The Be Happy Attitudes*. Did Bonhoeffer anticipate such a thing? Beatitude by beatitude, the visible gap between the disciples and the world's crowd widens. As if anticipating Schuller and surely appalled by the way Germans screamed their delight over Hitler, Bonhoeffer says, "The world shrieks 'Enjoy life,'" while the disciples grieve. Indeed, they become "strangers in the world, bothersome guests, disturbers of the peace."

What could be stranger than Bonhoeffer's profound understanding of mercy? He and his students had been hounded and threatened by an evil regime. Not imagining any other way to react to such a situation, we leap to the assumption that Bonhoeffer was an "assassin," for we can only yearn to win, to get even, to prove we're right and they're wrong.

But Bonhoeffer understood how the merciful shed their pride and take the shame of others on themselves. To be merciful, the merciful "cast away the most priceless treasure of human life, their personal dignity and honour. For the only honour and dignity they know is their Lord's own mercy,"[8] to which they owe their very lives. Yes, it's about an "irresistible love for the lowly, the sick, for those who are in misery, for those who are demeaned and abused"—and there were so many in 1935. The merciful, like their merciful Lord, seek out the sinful and guilty, those who've made themselves despicable in the world's eyes. No sin is beyond mercy. Could mercy be the healing balm for those we are so very sure think wrong about politics? Could mercy be the only medicine that might bring an end to division and violence in our world?

Matthew 5:21-48: Do Not Kill, Love Your Enemies

Sometimes readers of *The Cost of Discipleship* will thumb ahead to locate the spot where Bonhoeffer speaks "Do not kill" (Matthew 5:21) and "Love your enemies" (Matthew 5:44). If you think of him as a spy and an assassin (as in the title of the 2025 movie), you might hope he teases out some rationale to justify killing, or at least dealing firmly with, enemies.

Bonhoeffer had actually done this as a young pastor in Barcelona. Preaching on Matthew 5:39, he called it a "most serious misunderstanding" to apply Jesus's words uncritically to the present day. Pacifists (like Leo Tolstoy, whom he had in mind) are mistaken. It would be a painful decision, but in a time of war, he declared he would "be compelled to raise my hand against the enemy." God created nations and placed him in one with the absolute obligation to defend his family and people. "Love for my people will sanctify murder, will sanctify war."[9]

But things change, including his understanding God and Scripture. We can trace a definite evolution in Bonhoeffer's thinking and understanding of what Christianity required and so also in his own personal courage. In New York, he was befriended by Jean Lassere, a Frenchman, just months after French soldiers had killed Bonhoeffer's own brother Walter in World War I. Lassere took Jesus at his word on not killing and loving your enemy. Then, in 1933, Bonhoeffer made his astounding claim for a pastor holding two doctorates in theology, that he finally discovered the Bible, and that before he discovered the Bible he "had not yet become a Christian." He expressed "disgust and shame" over his earlier confused thinking and words.

From that point forward, he also took Jesus at his word. And Bonhoeffer's words are of immense value to any Christian today, and not merely on the question of whether one should kill to protect home and country. On the killing question, Bonhoeffer was clear: "Only God has power over life and death. . . . Murderers are liable to the judgment they themselves exercise."[10] He adds that this does not depend at all on the other person's "identity," a clear allusion to what Germans were then doing to the Jews. All depends not on the other person but on being a disciple of Jesus.

I love Bonhoeffer's meanderings on love, anger, and the enemy. For Jesus, anger itself crosses the boundary of not killing (Matthew 5:21-22). Anger is an assault, not only on the other person, but on God. "Angry words bursting out of us, which we take so lightly, reveal that we do not respect the other person, that we view ourselves to be superior." I sense that some of Bonhoeffer's father's psychiatric skills had been passed along to him. "Alienating oneself from another person causes alienation from God." In our season of so much rancor over politics, can we hear what Bonhoeffer is saying to us?

He delves deeply into loving enemies and never seeking retribution. "The followers of Jesus who experience injustice do not cling to their own rights as if they were possessions to be defended at all costs. Instead, they are completely free of such possessions and are bound to Jesus Christ." We recoil and object for various reasons, one being that we're sure this simply won't work.

Bonhoeffer believes it can work. Evil is seeking conflict, the resistance of a fight. And isn't it the case that when we combat evil, we can become what we are fighting against? Indeed, when evil meets "only patient endurance, its sting is drawn, and at last it meets an opponent who is more than its match."[11] I jotted "MLK" in the margins here, recalling the way Southern racists brutally attacked Black protesters led by Martin Luther King Jr., who won the day not by fighting back but by nonviolent resistance.

"To overcome enemies by loving them—that is God's will."[12] Sounds impossible, which may be the point. Loving an enemy is beyond our natural capacity; only God can achieve this in and through us. And it's not about whether such love is effective or whether it is reciprocated. "Love asks nothing in return, but seeks those who need it. And who needs our love more than those who are consumed with hatred and are utterly devoid of love? Who in other words deserves our love more than our enemy?"[13] Reread that. Make a copy and carry it around in your pocket. Bonhoeffer, I believe, got inside Jesus's head and heart and is speaking here for Jesus to you and me today.

When the first Gulf War had just broken out in 1990, I was watching *The MacNeil/Lehrer NewsHour*. A panel of clergy was asked about the faith community's thoughts on the war. One clergyman thundered strongly that God is with us and that we must triumph over the forces of evil. A second clergyman pretty much said the same thing. But the third, James Forbes, then a pastor in Harlem where Bonhoeffer's life had changed so dramatically, simply opened his Bible and read several verses from Matthew 5. When he got to "Love your enemies," he was interrupted by the first clergyman, who almost shouted, "That's not relevant now. We're at war!" Forbes calmly replied, "If it's not relevant now, it's never relevant."

Romans 12:16-21: Overcome Evil with Good

Relevance. Figuring out what time it is. The gospel is always the same, and yet the seasons of the world do change. Grace has its seasons. Luther thundered on the centrality and single necessity of grace. But he did so to people like himself who were very nervous and fastidious, certain they could never achieve enough to merit salvation. By Bonhoeffer's day, people took salvation for granted; they had forgotten or never learned that Luther himself was deadly serious about Christians living holy lives and the Church being a force for good in society. Bonhoeffer's *Discipleship* has been regarded as "a daring attempt to retrieve Luther from the shambles of his irrelevance in the Hitler era."[14]

Let's look at what Bonhoeffer does with some texts beyond the Sermon on the Mount. It's January 1938. Finkenwalde had been closed by the Gestapo four months earlier. Bonhoeffer's friend and fellow pastor Martin Niemöller had been arrested and imprisoned, just hours before Bonhoeffer showed up at his house to pay a visit! Incidentally, you can visit that house, with its displays of the resistance to Hitler that Niemöller led so courageously. And the church he pastored, St. Anne's, is right next door—so very small, given its mighty importance during the struggle with the Nazis, which goes to show what one, even small, church can do. Bonhoeffer had gone underground in northern Germany, determined to continue teaching and living in fellowship with the few stragglers left in the Confessing Church. To a tiny handful of the haggard faithful, he preached on Romans 12:16-21: "Do not claim to be wise. Do not repay anyone evil for evil.... Live peaceably with all.... Do not be overcome by evil, but overcome evil with good"—a text that would fit Forbes's category perfectly: "If it's not relevant now, it's never relevant."

"Do not claim to be wise." Bonhoeffer plays on this command to underline our human inability to comprehend mercy: "You may be very smart and competent people in your business, at your work, but there is one thing that by nature you do not know anything about at all... in the divine things of mercy or, much more, in how an enemy turns into a friend, how an enemy of God is overcome."[15] Who told people they could be wise? It was the devil who suggested they could be judges of good and evil. This "devil's gift of wisdom" is not to be embraced, "or otherwise human beings will devour each other."

God does not love us more than our enemies:

> Does God love our enemies less, having come for them, suffered for them, died for them as well as for us.... God suffers for their sake, experiences misery and pain for their sake; the Father has given his dear Son for them. Everything depends on this: that whenever we meet an enemy, we immediately think, this is someone whom God loves. God has given everything for this person.

Bonhoeffer is human, mentioning that his "blood boils" when he even sees a certain person, and he is "filled by a terrible, threatening anger." But then? He continues, "Now I have to be careful. Now I need to remember quickly: *mercy has happened to me*, not by human doing, no, but *by God*, and *for this person* Jesus Christ *died*—and suddenly everything changes."

To react otherwise is to open yourself to what the evil one wants to instill in you—that you also become evil. Then the winner is, yes, evil. We are to be peaceable, as the text pleads with us, "not only with *the peaceful*, but especially with those who do not want to let us live in peace." Do we flee from or avoid enemies? No, because "Jesus Christ was in the midst of his enemies. He wanted to be precisely there. This is where we also should be. This is what distinguishes us from all other sects and religions." Do we seek out those who think or live differently or even wrongly? Or do we prefer to isolate ourselves with others who require no effort to live in peace?

Luke 4:5-8: To You I Will Give

Two months after his ordination, Bonhoeffer preached a very short sermon to the students at the Technical College in Berlin, where he served as chaplain. His text? Luke 4:5-8, which begins, "The devil led him up and showed him in an instant all the kingdoms of the world." I'm surprised he doesn't mention the magnificent panoramic view from the top of a mountain looming above Barcelona called Tibidabo—taken from the Latin "To you I will give." When he was pastoring in Barcelona, he would climb that mountain and ponder the view while reflecting on the devil's offer to Jesus. "Jesus could have become the most glorious and powerful king of this world."[16]

Seeing all this in a flash, Jesus also understood that "for this rule he would have to pay a price that is too high for him. It would have come at the cost of his obedience to the will of God." What an intriguing reflection. If we saw some path to the greatest possible good, if we could snap our fingers and have our lives and even the life of the world turn out beautifully, wouldn't we jump at it?

I'm reminded of that ring of power in Tolkien's *The Lord of the Rings.* Whoever possesses and wears that ring can rule. The wicked, from Saruman to Gollum, pursue the ring for their vile purposes. But the noble and good, like Boromir, believe they could rule for the good. It is the wise Gandalf who feels that very temptation but understands that power corrupts even the least corruptible among us. The ring is to be destroyed. Tolkien's narrative embodies what Jesus's quest was all about: not seizing more power but defeating power itself with suffering love.

Judges 6–8: No Side Altars

We'll conclude this chapter with one of Bonhoeffer's greatest sermons, preached when he was just twenty-six years old in Berlin during February 1933. Somehow, the majority of Germans perceived the rise of the Nazis, the hatred and cruel treatment of the Jews, and preparations to launch another war as great blessings. This sermon, his first after Hitler had assumed power just one month earlier, was a profound reading of the story of Gideon in Judges 6–8. The very fact that he chose an Old Testament text in the climate of vicious anti-Semitism was brave.

Bonhoeffer sizes up the Gideon narrative as "a passionate story about God's derision for all those who are fearful and have little faith, all those who are much too careful, the worriers."[17] At the same time, and because of this, our story is, as theologian Dean G. Stroud writes, "a story of God's mocking human might, a story of doubt and of faith in this God who makes fun of human beings, who wins them over with this mockery and with love."

Ridiculously outnumbered and then instructed by God to send most of the few soldiers he had home, Gideon won the day—by God's power, not his own. And then when the people clamored to make him king and rule over them, he refused, rightly reminding them that for the people of God who follow faithfully, there is no human ruler. Only God rules. "In the church we have only one altar. . . . We don't have any side altars at which to worship human beings." The congregation must have trembled, or wanted to cheer, or slip away into hiding. Altars of the churches were already being draped in

Nazi swastikas, and Hitler not only ruled but was increasingly bathed in the aura of being god-like, an idol before whom all were to bow down.

Then Bonhoeffer named the one virtue that would be required but in short supply over the next decade: courage. "The thing that most hinders us from letting God be Lord, that is, from believing in God, is our cowardice." I wonder if Paul meant to include "courage" when he was ticking off his list of the fruits of the Spirit in Galatians 5.

I admire the way Bonhoeffer lifts up this character from biblical times and invites listeners to find him right here, right now: "Gideon asks, 'How can I deliver Israel?' This Gideon is someone we know isn't he? The call comes to our Protestant church," small, without influence, undistinguished, powerless, hopeless. Before shrugging the task off as impossible, Bonhoeffer reminds his people, and us, that it is God who does this calling: "Doesn't it drown out all your 'with what' questions?"

Bonhoeffer urges his congregants: "Never forget, even when your own powerlessness is grinding you down to the ground, that God has phenomenal, immeasurable, great plans for you. . . . Gideon conquers, the church conquers, we conquer, because faith alone conquers." Dean Stroud points out that the German for "conquers" is the verb *siegen*, an unmistakable echo of the Nazi slogan and salute, "Sieg heil!"

No mincing of words for Bonhoeffer! Yet it's the plainest possible sense of the biblical text that minces no words but rings out with a radical call for us to rise up boldly, courageously, and fearlessly, not measuring merely what we are sure we can get done but focused entirely on what God has asked, and can deliver, especially in times of crisis.

And when is this time of crisis? Now? Bonhoeffer's, as he delivered his white-hot lectures on the Baltic, might put yours in the shade. But every season of challenge is real, even if we think we're in a dull season. Isn't it during the time when the world and the life of faith seem settled that we need to be readying ourselves for the next crisis about to peer over the horizon?

Chapter 5

CHURCH/ RELIGIONLESS?

Bonhoeffer's wisdom on Christian community, his thoughts on why and how Church matters, and his enduring elucidation about what Scripture has to say about the mission of the Church are compelling—and would be even if he hadn't been leading the church during such a toxic, dangerous season. That he wrote and preached and acted when and where he did make his insights downright breathtaking. We would be wise to listen carefully and even rethink what Church is about today.

I am fascinated by the simple fact that Bonhoeffer thought so wisely about the Church and had (and continues to have) such an impact on it—for he grew up in a family that very rarely attended church. What was it that moved him, as a thirteen-year-old, to announce he'd decided to enter the ministry, to become a theologian? His family scoffed: "Look at the church. A more paltry institution one can hardly imagine." Dietrich blurted out his reply: "In that case, I shall reform it!"[1]

As a young college student, he traveled to Rome, and the wonder of worship and the church universal dawned on and delighted him. His first doctoral thesis was about the cruciality of the Church community, how you cannot be a Christian just for yourself but only as part of a larger body. And most impactful was the spiritual earthquake that his time with the Abyssinian Baptist Church in New York proved to be. In his short life, he stood in the pulpit, in front of the church, much more than he was ever out in the congregation!

Psalm 133:1: Life Together

Let's start in Finkenwalde. Bonhoeffer was enjoying life as pastor to two small German expatriate churches in London in 1935. But he heard a clear calling (from his mentor Barth among others) to return home and jump into the fray. While he'd been away, church leaders who pandered to the Nazis had come to wield so much influence over the seminaries that pro-Hitler, anti-Semitic teachings were all would-be clergy were exposed to. So a small minority, those aligned with the Confessing Church, stole away to the Baltic peninsula to start their own seminary and asked Bonhoeffer to serve as its director. The fledgling seminary hung on for just over two years before going underground after the Gestapo shut it down.

This was a season of inspired genius for Bonhoeffer. His lectures on the Sermon on the Mount were published as *The Cost of Discipleship*, in which we find a daring vision of church. Also, he gifted the world and us with another little gem of a book, *Life Together*, something of a report on the experiment in Christian living that was the seminary at Finkenwalde. Students didn't come just to study. Bonhoeffer dreamed of their life together in prayer, discipline, and service—a genuinely Christian community. I love my friend Ben Gosden's remark: "I think *Life Together* is even more challenging than *Cost of Discipleship* because of the requirement to do discipleship in the context of community. It's much easier if I can just die to Christ daily all by myself."

Bonhoeffer's first words in *Life Together* were, not surprisingly, God's words: "How very good and pleasant it is when kindred live together in unity!" (Psalm 133:1). From there, he plunges right in: "The Christian cannot simply take for granted the privilege of living among other Christians."[2] We come together not just to enjoy one another's company, but for the sake of Jesus Christ. Christian community is grace. I wonder whether Bonhoeffer knew that John Wesley counted Christian fellowship as one of his "means of grace." Hearing his words against the backdrop of Nazi oppression is so poignant: "It is grace, nothing but grace, that we are still permitted to live in the community of Christians today"—words he suggested should be uttered on our knees.

"The physical presence of other Christians is a source of incomparable joy and strength to the believer." These words move me when I think of what that small handful of courageous seminary students was facing. Bonhoeffer knew they would need one another in the dark days to come—as we always need one another. Bonhoeffer shows us how joy and strength happen because we speak of God to one another, and how, when we are together, we anticipate what heaven will be like. For his seminarians, as for any of us who live in close quarters with others, when we faithfully cope with quirks and habits of others, and engage in the simple labor of survival, our egos undergo some humbled healing.

Indeed, those seeking some emotional high or an extraordinary experience in community will be disappointed. The Church isn't ideal, but real, "a divine reality." Those who fantasize about a perfect community that suits them are the very ones who destroy community. They become demanding judges, yet the only constructive and faithful basis for community is thankfulness.

Christian community isn't just me and some other people trying to be tight. I love the way Bonhoeffer's great biographer Charles Marsh describes why Jesus Christ is how community happens or doesn't: "Without Christ, humanity would know neither God nor the neighbor, for the way to the other is always constricted by the ego. However, Christ opens up the way to the other by pulling the self out of itself into life with others and by drawing the person into faithful togetherness."[3] Focusing on Christ transforms community and can land you in a very different kind of community.

Life Together provides guidelines for how to talk, and not talk, to one another. He reflects on James 4:11 and Ephesians 4:29, noticing that we often "combat our evil thoughts most effectively if we absolutely refuse to allow them to be verbalized,"[4] thus acknowledging the apparently unavoidable human weakness of hatching judgmental thoughts. Therefore, Bonhoeffer devised what he called "the decisive rule of all community life," that you never talk about anyone who is not in the room. As a pastor, I have devised what I call "the James Howell improvement upon the rule of Dietrich Bonhoeffer"—which is that you never talk about anyone who is not in the room unless you are praising them. Oh, and then he diagnoses the pious veneer we sometimes paste onto our talking about others: “Talking about others in secret is not allowed even under the pretense of help and goodwill.” All the time, we whisper, “Oh, I’m so concerned about Susan” or “Did you hear what John did? We should pray for him.” And then there’s the laughable default remark, more common in the Southern United States: “Bless her heart.”

Like the early Methodists, the students of Finkenwalde confessed their sins to one another. Bonhoeffer understands why this is essential. It’s very scriptural! But also “in confession there takes place a breakthrough to community. Sin wants to be alone with people. The more lonely people become, the more destructive the power of sin over them. The more deeply they become entangled in it, the more unholy is their loneliness.” Indeed, when sin is confessed to another person, its power is broken. Clearly, Bonhoeffer’s vision for the church community is very different from our gathering with people with whom we like to exchange pleasantries.

Psalm 65:2: In Silence

He was writing for a church in Finkenwalde where everyone lived in close quarters together. Would that make deep community easier or harder? Bonhoeffer mapped out what a day together should look like. At Finkenwalde, the morning began with prayer, which they would do together, yet in silence! How fitting is it that today, in the Polish city of Szczecin, a lovely Garden for Silence and Meditation is located in the place where the seminary once stood. It's labyrinth-like: You walk in a large circle, sit on benches, and ponder quotes from Bonhoeffer as you weigh his words and our life together today.

As I dove into his section of *Life Together* on how prayer begins the day, I wondered what text he would fix his (and our) attention upon. Not one, but a little catalog of texts flow from his pen, from Psalms 5, 88, 57, 119, 63, and 46, then veering into Lamentations, Ephesians, Genesis, and Mark. Did he have a concordance as he prepared? Maybe. Or maybe, like so many who are blessed from a long life of regular immersion in the Bible, his mind simply flitted from one to the next. You're not there yet, I suspect, but you can start, even without a physical concordance. Google has its spiritual uses!

Can we conceive of our prayer as something we do with others? You and I, reader, are not physically present as we read, but if we engage in shared habits when separate, we grow into a spiritual communion that changes everything when we are physically together—or if we never meet each other! What an immense encouragement!

Church is listening for God's Word, not critiquing the preacher or seeking agreement, or hanging out with people who share our individual lifestyle and biases. As we saw in chapter 3, Church is shaped best by silence, listening for God and listening for suffering in others and in the world. When we read and pray the Psalms in particular, we do so as one with Jesus, the one who suffered and takes our suffering upon himself. The Psalms "cast every difficulty and tribulation upon God: 'We can no longer bear them, take them away and bear them yourself, for you alone can handle suffering.' "

Suffering is something we don't handle well in Christian community. We pity the sufferer. Or, like Job's friends, we blame the sufferer, even under the guise of concern. Or we trot out trite little remarks such as "Everything happens for a reason" or "God won't give you more than you can bear." Bonhoeffer suggests we can handle suffering in the good company of others, not because we are great caregivers, but for the sake of Jesus Christ, who suffered and bears suffering. "We must learn to regard human beings less in the light of what they do and neglect to do, and more in terms of what they suffer"[5]—this latter idea eerily sounding alike a prophecy of trauma-based therapy, which wouldn't become a thing until half a century after Bonhoeffer's death.

2 Corinthians 5:20: Ambassadors for Christ

Ever reliant on the Word of God, Bonhoeffer preached his very first sermon as the new pastor of the church in London in 1933, not shrinking back from naming the elephant in the room—a situation we've all faced at least once in a while and sometimes all too often. "Every change of pastors in a congregation is bound up with all sorts of human emotions."[6]

Then he explored 2 Corinthians 5:20, where Paul clearly invites the church not to get hung up on personalities, whether you like the new guy, whether you miss the old guy. "We get stuck in our very personal feelings, but we should be encouraged to see something much larger, which does not concern persons at all...but rather concerns the mission that is entrusted to both of them, no matter who they are." It's the preaching rather than the preacher. "We are ambassadors"—*we*, as in all of us in the church, which was never designed to be entertainment like the cinema or a playground for our feelings, but the place "where God's word is obediently received and believed."

How gutsy was his observation, based entirely on Scripture and not on the people he, of course, did not yet know, that some churchgoers prefer things to be cozy and comfy instead of "letting ourselves be disturbed by the holy restlessness of the powerful Lord God." I'm with Bonhoeffer when he says to pastors: "We need to know that the congregation is shouldering the burden with us, helping us, standing by us, pointing out our mistakes and praying for us." Indeed, "many a pastor has failed because he or she wanted to carry the congregation, but the congregation did not carry the pastor."

We saw in chapter 1 how Bonhoeffer opened up the heart of 1 Corinthians 13, especially the little historical fact that the church grew and thrived in a hostile culture largely because social divisions crumbled in the Christian community. Pagans were shocked and impressed that masters and their slaves as well as estranged siblings were no longer at odds with one another. They were one community. His first paragraph in *Life Together* reminds us that Jesus loved and told us to love our enemies—and so they too are in church with us.

This shapes the Church's political role in society. Ours is not to baptize this or that political party or agenda. Ours is to "remind the state of its duty to care for justice, order, and peace. In this the church may not think it is the better politician. Good policy requires political competency, detailed knowledge, and training . . . abilities that do not automatically come with the Christian faith."[7] Indeed, the church must "keep asking the government whether its actions can be justified as legitimate state actions, that is, actions that create law and order, not lack of rights and disorder." The Church keeps its distance from the state not to be silenced but to exercise its prophetic function.

Matthew 5:44: The Church's Love of Enemies

Bonhoeffer's reflections on the Church grew shrewder and more pointed as the situation in Germany, and the relentless pressure on the churches, grew worse. Would the church pervert itself by caving in? Would the church be shut down? Would pastors and Christians actually lose their lives? What was it like to go to church, and especially to be a pastor, in a nation where Hitler spoke so mockingly of the faithful churches and their classic theology of the Christ of Scripture, where you could be arrested or lose your life for simply adhering to the straight Gospel versus the sham pseudotheology of the Third Reich?

There's nothing casual or convenient about churchgoing in such a place and time. Huddled in the cold for worship with his little band at Finkenwalde, Bonhoeffer staked out an astonishing, seemingly impossible mission for the church, which is and will always be its mission: "The church-community has a very real impact on the life of the world. It gains space for Christ."[8] We do not flee or hide, even in such a season of persecution. We stay in the world

> not because of the God-given goodness of the world, nor even because of their responsibility for the course the world takes. They are to remain in the world solely for the sake of the body of the

> Christ who became incarnate. . . . They are to remain in the world in order to engage the world in a frontal assault.

That assault is not a violent one; it's not about winning. In the very first paragraph of *Life Together*, he reminds us that "Jesus Christ lived in the midst of his enemies. In the end, all his disciples abandoned him. On the cross, he was all alone."[9] "Love your enemies" was just one of many very clear, very difficult, and yet very hopeful moments in Jesus's Sermon on the Mount. What would it look like if churches took Matthew 5–7 as their charter or strategic plan?

For Bonhoeffer, it was the unlikely scriptural text, the one hardest to live by, that shaped what the Church was about. Anyone could find an enemy or two within the church, and their little circle of a church lived encircled by literal enemies. Theirs was to love—not because that was a strategy that would work, but because Jesus told us to love our enemies. Jesus loved his enemies. We are to be Jesus in and for the world.

Church strives to be genuine community, less an institution. In his final months, Bonhoeffer sketched out an outline for a book, something of a manifesto for what Church could and might soon be. He'd moved beyond his longtime vision of church as a structure with four sides open outward to the world. In his outline, that building collapses, leaving only the community in exile, in solidarity with all the outsiders, the ostracized. Pastors would have no privileges or security but would live in the world, ready to serve as needed with other Christians. He dreamed of a church striving to live out the simple stuff in Scripture. A church for the weak, the lost, the wounded. A church that doesn't kowtow to any state or political ideology.

Religionless Christianity

With this in mind, we turn now to Bonhoeffer's most radical and memorable ideas about the future of the church, all under the explosive idea of "religionless Christianity." What could possibly be more timely for us today, with religion held almost in contempt and churches selling out to political ideologies, than what Bonhoeffer was reckoning with during his final months in prison?

It's intriguing to me that a thinker like Bonhoeffer, a longtime bestseller in the field of religion, managed to popularize the word *religionless*—and in a positive way. A religionless Christianity? Isn't Christianity a religion? I know that I was drawn to Bonhoeffer as a young man precisely because he seemed done with religion. Personally, I wasn't done with religion; I'd never really started! I didn't know much "religion," and I wasn't enamored with what I did know about it. Religion seemed to me to be staid, dull, with lots of guilt and intellectual laziness. Couldn't I get Jesus without all the religion?

For a year or two, I thought maybe I could. I'd fallen in with a group of passionate, joyful Christians who met in an old house in the backyard of an old, cathedral-like marvel of a church building—which I had never personally entered. No one spoke of it this way, but there was symbolism in that. Unlike the routine churchgoers who dressed in their finery and mumbled through prayers and hymns and yawned through sermons, we were alive, all in, and joyful. Pulsating Christianity without the dead religion.

My friend Lillian Daniel has written ingenuously about what all pastors have to address: people who claim to be spiritual without being religious. We pastors get it, but we yawn or fire back with our critique—that such spirituality is usually pretty vapid and self-indulgent, with no accountability, more about me and my pet wishes about God than anything challenging or truthful. It's pretty sunsets and warm fuzzy moments, without having to mix it up with prickly people or doing anything hard or sacrificial for God.

Bonhoeffer too would have scoffed at such a spirituality. I dare anybody who's "spiritual but not religious" to get past the second page of *The Cost of Discipleship*. This is no easy chair, convenient Christianity—and I don't mean with Bonhoeffer, but with the Jesus you might wish to have if he'd been a little more laid back and comforting.

Amos 5:23: Take Away the Noise of Your Songs

Let's ponder where and when Bonhoeffer wrote about a religionless Christianity. He was in prison for courageously standing up against Hitler and the Nazis. And he was all but alone in doing so. How had "religion," with its religious leaders and religious people, reacted to the rise of this führer, his warmongering, and his murderous hatred of the Jews? They nodded and cheered. They *heil*-ed this Hitler, fawning over him as their savior. They averted their gaze, or they played their part in the abuse and execution of millions of Jews.

Religion had proven to be an abysmal failure when it was needed the most. Religion—that is, the Christian churches—were not merely impotent in the face of rampant evil. The churches were also complicit, in league with the Nazis. Religion in Germany blessed what was unfolding and blasphemously attached the name of the Lord to what was the very antithesis of all that Lord was about.

Religion's failure was long in the making. What vapid, watered-down message had been preached, and what innocuous, misguided theology had been taught to generations of little boys and girls and their parents that then blinded them to what was sheer perversity? This is religion? Imagine all the worship services and group discussions where the beast of German nationalism was being fed and growing ever stronger. Religion's dying was the inevitable result of religion's own miserable failures and sin.

There was nothing peculiar about the religion of Germany in the 1930s and 1940s. It seems as if every age suffers from religion gone bad. Within the Bible itself, we read of God's readiness to wash God's hands of religion. The prophets Amos, Hosea, and Jeremiah share God's heart in loathing the noise of worship and pretend piety in Israel. Jesus weeps over Jerusalem at the feast of Passover and then strides into the temple, overturns the tables, and declares the temple will and should be destroyed before long.

Jesus Christ himself clearly exposed the failure of religion. Religious authorities convicted him, and the religious people cried out, "Crucify him!" Jesus was the ultimate religious disappointment, not at all what religious people then or now expected from God. Religion, then and now, doesn't always deliver light and love to the soul. In our day, Richard Rohr wisely points out, "For the untransformed self, religion is the most dangerous temptation of all,"[10] as it seems to foster judgment, meanness, division, and rage.

Of course, the twisted masquerade that religion was in Germany stands forever as a loud and dire warning to every generation of Christians in every place. Is whatever happening in our country presently at odds with what we know quite clearly from Scripture? Are we as individual Christians and as churches stumbling into buying any lies shoveled toward us from politicians? Is our political ideology the idol, the god we bow down to, that we believe really will deliver the goods and be our salvation? What will the next generation make of today's church? Will they be proud of us for our courage and determination to stick with the real Jesus? Or will they shudder in embarrassment, concluding we remade Jesus in the image of the politicians because we didn't bother to wrestle with the authentic Jesus or were just too chicken to follow him during dark days?

In his very last letters from prison, just weeks before his execution, Bonhoeffer tellingly wrote about "how little I miss going to church."[11] In his oft-quoted letter of April 1944 to Eberhard, when he was first speculating that "we are moving toward a completely religionless time," he confessed, "What keeps gnawing at me is the question, what is Christianity, or who is Christ actually for us today?" Having witnessed and suffered at the hands of what Christianity really is not, Bonhoeffer came to understand what it really is, and who Christ really is as a simple path, exemplified by all we've seen already in his approach to Scripture.

Or maybe we should say the *way* he let himself and his world be approached by Scripture. We get the order wrong so often, flipping through pages of Scripture to find a boost or help. Or the sort of thing the cartoonist Charles Schulz (of Peanuts fame) had in mind when he drew a young woman trying to get the attention of a young man with his Bible propped open. His response in the caption? "Don't bother me. I'm looking for a verse of Scripture to back up one of my preconceived notions." To read the Bible with Bonhoeffer, we do so on the lookout for any preconceptions, however lovely or tried and true they seem, and we shed them, shove them aside, and try as best we can to read with an open mind, an open life, even an open schedule for the day and the rest of our days.

The major problem with religion is that it has been constructed in a way that leads us to expect that religion's whole reason to exist is to provide comfort or assistance for me, and maybe others too. Religion as Bonhoeffer knew it, and as we still experience today, is so very individualistic. Sermons offer little nuggets of advice to the individual about how to be good, or how to slake your spiritual thirst, or how to minimize your worries and fears. Bonhoeffer was in a close relationship with the God who was far larger than all that, one who made us for community, one who did not wish for us to be afraid, but courageous, mature. He knew his Bible, in whose pages "repentance" isn't apologizing or groveling or gritting our teeth and trying to do better. Rather, repentance is "not in the first place thinking about one's own needs, problems, sins and fears, but allowing oneself to be caught up into the way of Jesus Christ."

Philippians 4:6: Fear Not!

The fear factor in religion is worth reflecting on. The most frequent command in the Bible? "Fear not." Mind you, it can feel like piling on. You have your fears, your anxieties. Then you turn to Scripture, which admonishes you to "Fear not" or "Do not be anxious," and your fears and anxieties tighten a little harder, don't they?[12] Critics of Christianity, whether we mean those titans of skepticism like Freud, Marx, and Nietzsche or maybe people you know who scoff at the idea of religion, think of religious people as fearful, scurrying into the church hoping God will protect them from whatever frightens them.

Bonhoeffer offers us some refreshing, novel thoughts on our fears, particularly our fear that hard questions we ask about God, or from critics of God and the life of faith, might just pull out that one wrong Jenga block, causing the tower of religion to come tumbling down. With time to think and nothing much to do but write letters, Bonhoeffer focused on his "religionless" theme and owned the reality that over many centuries, the world had "come of age"; it had "matured." Once upon a time, a storm or disease or any misfortune would be chalked up to God's wrath or the devil's wiles. But humanity had learned about meteorology and medicine and therefore we had newer, better explanations for why bad things happened. Just as a person (hopefully) matures by understanding more of the world and how to function wisely within it, so humanity had come of age.

Religion, if anything, fed humanity's immaturity, suggesting either that we can't know God's hidden purpose or fleeing from new knowledge as threatening to God and faith, which Bonhoeffer called "an attempt to put a grown-up man back into adolescence, i.e. to make him dependent on things on which he is, in fact, no longer dependent."[13] In a great image, Bonhoeffer notices that God gets "smuggled in somewhere" to explain what baffles us or to solve our problems or fix what we can't fix. Or we fear God is getting squeezed out, so we smuggle God in.

Ephesians 4:6: God Is Above, Through and In All Things

For Bonhoeffer, God is in all things, not just religious things. God is everywhere, not just a genie or a heavenly repairman we call in as needed. A lot of religious silliness, or immaturity, fades away if we can rethink God with Bonhoeffer. It's a child who prays for God to protect them and their loved ones; many carry this long into adulthood and are shocked when anything bad happens, concluding there is no God, or God is acting out some vendetta against them. But the mature have grown-up views, leaving their naivete behind. I'm amused by Jeffrey Pugh's witty remark on Bonhoeffer's point: "We do not need recourse to God when nature destroys our homes; we have insurance."[14]

If religion nurtures in us the notion that God is our protector, that God is there to answer our prayers, then let's dispense with religion, for religion's God is an utter failure at doing God's job. Let's be clear: Bonhoeffer discerned the terrible problem with thinking of God in this way. He simply names reality, which contradicts any simplistic notion of God as protector. He also helps us see that this is precisely what Scripture reveals to us about God and our life with God. God is in all things. God isn't a 911 responder or a doctor's helper. So many give up on God because some problem bedevils them because they've been misshapen to believe God is a hovering protector.

Bonhoeffer's embrace of humanity's maturity, of a world come of age, also liberates us from fretting over those critics who question Christianity. The hardest questions against our faith aren't out there but in Scripture itself! Jesus asks why God would abandon him. Job launches a searing criticism against God for failing to help or even listen. Nietzsche, Freud, the *DaVinci Code*, or that teacher or professor you had in school who ridiculed Christianity have got nothing on Scripture itself!

On first glance, faithful readers shrink back when they find Bonhoeffer saying things like "God would have us know that we must live as those who manage their lives without God."[15] But what do parents strive for with their children? A lasting dependence? Parents long for their children to mature into adults who don't need parents as they did when they were toddlers or even adolescents. There's a deeper, different kind of love a person discovers for parents after becoming independent.

It's also worth pondering how often the Bible shares almost as much about God being absent as God being present. Samuel Terrien spoke of God's "elusive presence." Job talks for thirty-five chapters with no divine reply. The book of Esther does not mention God, not even once. The story of Joseph (Genesis 37–50) implies God is hiding behind the curtains, impacting what's happening visibly on stage, but the writer seems reticent to claim too much, delighting in the maybe. Rabbi David Wolpe points out that "there is not a single supernatural miracle in the entire story of David, the longest continuous narrative about a human being in the entire Hebrew Bible."[16]

I'm moved and haunted by Bonhoeffer's most enigmatic yet powerful thoughts: "The world that has come of age is more god-less and perhaps just because of that closer to God than the world not yet come of age."[17] Reread that. Ponder that. Take hope in that. Instead of fretting about growing secularism or the banal culture we find ourselves in, we might just discover a newer, richer closeness to God.

Think of the welcoming of questions pointed against faith in God. Noting progress in science, Bonhoeffer claims, "Human beings have learned to manage all important issues by themselves, without recourse to 'Working hypothesis: God.'" The Church has recoiled against human explanations for things—foolishly. The world had witnessed the embarrassing Scopes Monkey Trial in America, where a teacher was charged and found guilty of teaching things we now know are simply facts. The Church needn't fear the progress of knowledge; we should celebrate. Otherwise, God becomes increasingly irrelevant or gets "smuggled in somewhere." God isn't in what you don't know, but in what you know, your real world; God doesn't dip a miraculous finger in here or there.

In 2002, the world-famous scientist Stephen Hawking published *The Theory of Everything*, a marvelous book that declared we can explain how everything came to be without recourse to God. Nervous church members called me, a bit panicked, asking me to respond. I laughed and pointed out that even though I majored in chemistry and physics, the odds of me outsmarting Hawking in a debate were zero. Quickly, I came to understand that even God was pleased with Hawking's conclusion, as Bonhoeffer would have been. God does not have to exist. God doesn't make it so that you have no choice but to believe. God is love. Love doesn't compel. Love risks and is open to being rejected. Jesus never compelled anybody to believe. Paul preached, celebrated any and all who welcomed the gospel, and then moved on.

None of this wisdom makes sense without remembering that for Bonhoeffer, religionless Christianity has as its focal point the crucified Christ. Notice how his earlier words on the world's coming of age continue:

> God would have us know that we must live as those who manage their lives without God. . . . God consents to be pushed out of the world and onto the cross; God is weak and powerless in the world and in precisely this way, and only so, is at our side and helps us.

Or as the older, more familiar translation puts it, "Only the suffering God can help." Jesus's cry of abandonment as he's being executed by his own religion reveals the ultimate truth about God, religion, and us: When we suffer, when we feel forsaken by God, when our religion has failed us, we are not far from God, but very close to God.

And so, our religious lives are simplified just as we discover that nothing can separate us from God. "Our being Christian today will be limited to two things: prayer, and righteous action among men." We will find a new language, "perhaps quite [a] nonreligious language, but liberating and redeeming like Jesus's language, so that people will be alarmed and yet overcome by its power—the language of a new righteousness and truth, a language proclaiming that God makes peace with humankind and that God's kingdom is drawing near."

Chapter 6

DEATH AND LEGACY

Charles Marsh opened his great biography with a revealing, luminous moment from an unusual childhood: "Dietrich Bonhoeffer and his twin sister, Sabine, lay awake at night trying to imagine eternity."[1] They were obsessed with the word *ewigkeit*, "eternity." Dietrich envisioned himself on his deathbed, with his family and friends hovering. He planned then what his last words would be and practiced them out loud. His dream was to welcome death when it arrived. He adored the little ditty his mother would sing: "When at night I go to bed, fourteen angels round my stead."

Precocious, this child? Was he the theological equivalent of Luke Skywalker? "The force is strong with this one"? He had premonitions of an early death. When he was twenty-three, he told a cousin, "I will not grow old; I'll die when I'm forty years old."[2] Close. He was thirty-nine on April 9, 1945, when he was hanged in the Flossenbürg prison camp. On a bitter cold, icy day, I stood in the camp's courtyard where he and six others were executed. Haunting. Sad. Strangely beautiful. I felt some of the weight of all fallen humanity and the tragedy of chance and timing, recalling that if they had waited just four more weeks, he'd have been liberated with all the others when Germany surrendered. The surprise is that he survived as long as he did, given his constant and courageous opposition to Hitler, the Reich's tamed church leaders, and the brutal treatment of the Jews.

To ponder the reality of death is the way to wisdom, and a crucial piece of understanding what Christianity has to offer. But for a child to lie awake at night and imagine dying? I'd have been troubled to learn any of my children were doing that at age six or eight or twelve.

And yet Bonhoeffer was not just an early bloomer spiritually. He grew up in a world where you could not deny or avert your gaze from the specter of death, including premature death. Bonhoeffer was just eight when the mindless, unwinnable carnage that was World War I began. His own brother Walter was killed, as were cousins and neighbors he knew. Political assassinations were common. When foreign minister Walther Rathenau was killed, Bonhoeffer heard the gunfire from his classroom. With the outbreak of World War II, more friends were dying in battle, including Franz Jägerstätter (who was made a saint in 2007 by Pope Benedict XVI) and more than half his seminary students from Finkenwalde. We can't count the number of times the Nazis threatened to kill him.

Bonhoeffer understood all too well that death isn't just the end for the deceased. There is a kind of death of the spirit for those left behind, those who hear the news and are never the same. The words of George Santayana's poem ring true: "With you a part of me hath passed away,... and I am grown much older in a day."[3] Bonhoeffer shared in the intense grief of his parents after the death of Walter. His father, Karl, had always been an upbeat man but turned permanently stoic after the telegram came announcing his son was gone. He would storm from the room at the mere mention of Walter's name. Bonhoeffer's mother was even more stricken. She moved out of the house to spare her children from seeing and hearing her utter misery. She hardly got out of bed for a month, holding Walter's last letter to her in her hand.

Remembering the depth of their sorrow, Bonhoeffer did all he could to sound upbeat and well when he wrote to his parents from prison. It would be easy to cite his chipper messages and conclude he was one of those spiritual titans you might have known who maintain a sunny disposition even during seasons of great loss. But in his letters to his closest friend, Bethge, he reports on mood swings, the abysmal food and conditions, and his struggles to cope in the depths of depression.

Psalm 90: Teach Us to Number Our Days

Back in chapter 1, we listened in on Bonhoeffer's lovely homily at the funeral of his grandmother, Julie. He spoke fondly of her, but he was also working his text, Psalm 90. Several of its verses reflect on the passing of time. He pondered how those words fit her long life: "She came from another time, from another age of the spirit—and that age does *not* pass with her into the grave. That heritage, for which we thank her, is binding upon us today."[4] Unlike many twenty-nine-year-olds, Bonhoeffer did not jauntily believe newer is better. The psalm clings to what is old, tried, and tested, and with regard to his grandmother, Bonhoeffer was speaking of her and her age's "inviolability of justice" and "the free word of a free person, the binding character of one's word, clarity and sobriety in speech, uprightness," explicitly mentioning her sorrow over the treatment of the Jews and the bold way she stood for and with them. Such ancient wisdom that bound him still binds us.

Of course, as a Christian, he was comforted by a bold hope. Building on verse 12, "Teach us to number our days that we may apply our hearts to wisdom," Bonhoeffer acknowledged that "we, too, must one day depart," that there is a "limit" to life. Wisdom is not only knowing our limitedness but also "knowing that beyond that limit is the God who is from eternity to eternity, into whose hands we fall, whether we choose to or not, in whose hands she is now lifted up in eternity." Notice that "eternity" lands three times in that single sentence—that favorite word of his as a child when he would imagine death. He even asks God for a special gift for his grandmother—"that she may see in eternity what is covered and buried here beneath sin and death, that she may see in all clearness and peace the eternal countenance of God in Jesus Christ." Two more eternities there!

We think of Bonhoeffer as this radical Christian (which as we've seen he really wasn't, or if he was, then we've watered it down) or as this courageous foe of Hitler (which of course he was, although he was neither a spy nor an assassin). And he came to regret some uncertainties along the way and never having fully arrived at clarity on things.

We would be wise to look to Bonhoeffer to answer that largest of all existential questions: When death comes, as it inevitably will, will we tremble before this grim reaper or welcome death as a friend? The world averts its gaze from death. The world lives in denial of death. The world rushes about trying to stay a step ahead of death. The world sentimentalizes death, or pities the dying and the survivors.

Christianity has the resources to face and even welcome death. We are not freaked out by death beacause the focal point of all that God has been about in creation, history, and my own personal life and yours is a man of sorrows hanging on a cross. In his last letter to Maria, Bonhoeffer wrote what we all hope to be able to say and can, by God's grace, be empowered to say: "My past life is brim-full of God's goodness, and my sins are covered by the forgiving love of Christ crucified."[5]

2 Corinthians 5:10: All Must Appear Before the Judgment Seat

And so, in a sermon he preached as a young man (as we recall, of course, he was never *not* a young man), he explores a passage that could certainly feel threatening: "All of us must appear before the judgment seat of Christ" (2 Corinthians 5:10). Wisely, without skirting the reality of judgment, Bonhoeffer understands this verse in the light of all Scripture and the overflow of mercy in God's heart: "God does not want human beings to be afraid, not even of the Last Judgment.... God sends us the word about the judgment only so that we will reach out more passionately, more hungrily for the promise of God's grace."[6] How easily he could have wagged a finger of warning against his parishioners and, even more, against the Nazis.

I'm reminded of the great insight of another German, Gerhard Lohfink, who fathomed how judgment truly is mercy:

> When we encounter God in death we will for the first time recognize with full clarity who we really are. God has no need to sit in judgment on us, to harangue us.... Our eyes will be opened to behold our own selves. We ourselves will judge and condemn the evil in ourselves.[7]

We will face our victims, some of whom we simply failed to help. We will realize the long-term impact of our actions (or inaction). Death will be an encounter with truth—and that truth will set us free when it dawns on us how gargantuan and tender is the mercy that forgives, heals, and redeems all of that. So yes, there is accountability, and that is good news, as we ultimately discover what we do in this life matters and that the mercy is even deeper the more we understand just that.

Psalm 62: God's Times of Salvation

So let's ask how Scripture nurtured in Bonhoeffer a kind of joyful courage, not the courage to speak out against Hitler, but the courage to live without being terrified by death. What do we tell young children? Face your fears! I love his friend Eberhard's observation: "He liked thinking about death.... To him death was neither grievous nor alien."[8] But he never thought about death in a vacuum. An open Bible was always the lookout point from which he pondered death and eternity (his lifelong favorite, *ewigkeit*). After all, isn't immersion in Scripture a long exercise in thinking about death?

The Psalms, of course, were daily companions in his life. Every morning he prayed a psalm or two. When his seminarians worshipped together each morning, they prayed Psalms. He had to have known most of them by heart, for a familiar psalm finds its way into your mind and heart as God's word in any and all situations.

When hearing of the horrors of *Kristallnacht*, that terrible torrent of violence on November 9, 1938, when synagogues were destroyed, Jewish shops and homes were burned, and Jews were killed fleeing in the streets, Bonhoeffer turned to Psalm 74:8, "They have set fire to all the houses of God in the land," and wrote the date in the margin. Then he added an exclamation point to the next verse: "There is no prophet to preach. How long, O God, shall the foe blaspheme?" If you'd like to adopt the noblest possible goal for the spiritual life, it might be storing up a trove of psalms in your heart so that when anything, sorrowful or cheerful, happens, your mind can retrieve just the word required.

Jesus, of course, did just that, didn't he? On the cross, he didn't make up some extemporaneous prayer. He went to Psalm 22, "My God, why have you forsaken me?" and then to Psalm 31, "Into your hands I commit my spirit." Bonhoeffer saw Jesus as the model, the pioneer of the one who lives in the face of death with Scripture as provider of courage and hope. Surely, like Bonhoeffer, Jesus had his own premonitions of death. Mary must have told him of Simeon's prophecy (Luke 2:34). Just as Bonhoeffer was hounded by the Gestapo, Jesus was hounded by Herod ("that fox" in Luke 13:32). And Jesus somberly told his disciples on multiple occasions that he was not long for this world.

We might learn from Bonhoeffer how the Psalms and silence ready us for death. As a twenty-two-year-old assistant pastor in Barcelona, he preached an elegant sermon on Psalm 62:1—a profound reflection on silence, why we avoid it even as we desperately need it. Instead of talking, in silence we can see God, the "other." Silence "means waiting, waiting for the Other to say something to us. Being silent before God means making room for God so that he may speak the first and last word about us."

Isn't that "last word" about salvation? In Europe in those days, fear of a sudden death was prevalent, inducing constant anxiety. Bonhoeffer called this "a mark of our times" that "we live in fear that we may suddenly find ourselves before the Eternal." There's *ewigkeit* again! But his text, Psalm 62, reminds us that what comes in the silence is salvation:

> God's times are times of salvation. God has an answer ready, and this answer is one and the same to whomever it is given: to the woman who has put behind her the hustle and bustle of everyday life, to the sick man who comes before God in his misery, to the one who is mourning the loss of a loved one, and to all who are guilt-laden. To man and woman, old person and child, God speaks his winning word: I love you. . . . If our soul has found the way to him, then he saves us, as sure as he is God.[9]

Psalm 119: I Am Given Time for the Grace of God

Let's listen to one more of the Psalms, Bonhoeffer's favorite. Psalm 119 is an elaborate acrostic: in Hebrew, the first letter of the first eight verses is the first letter of the alphabet, then the first letter of the next eight verses is the second letter, and so on through Hebrew's twenty-two letters, 176 verses praising God, whom the New Testament calls Alpha and Omega, literally from A to Z. Very cleverly, he sent messages to others in the underground using this same acrostic device he'd learned from Scripture!

He wrote a long, lovely meditation on this long, lovely psalm during the days when he taught seminarians at Finkenwalde. Among the psalm's themes is time. God creates time, God gives us time, God takes time for us:

> Life is the time of grace, death is judgment. Therefore, life is divine benefaction because I am given time for the grace of God. Such time is given as long as the word of God is with me. To hold on to this word is life from God that is affirmed.[10]

Notice that the way he thinks of God's Word as a companion during this passing of time and how Scripture sustains him and affirms his life has a sacredness to it.

Verse 19 particularly enthralled him: "I am a sojourner on the earth" (or we might translate it "stranger"). As one who moved often from place to place and never felt secure anywhere, Bonhoeffer felt these words were like a mirror of his existence. And yet he suggests that this sense of being a sojourner (as in the hymn we sing, "Guide me, O thou great Jehovah, pilgrim through this barren land"[11]) is a spiritual reality for us all. "When God's Word first encountered me, it made me a stranger on this earth."[12] Fascinating. Scripture doesn't make you feel at home, but instead induces a kind of restlessness, an awareness of dislocation. On realizing he'd been made a stranger on earth, Bonhoeffer muses, "Therefore, I confess that I cannot remain here, that my given time is brief," which isn't bad news, but simple reality, driving us into the eternal arms of a merciful God.

But Bonhoeffer is wary of those who have "too much heaven on their minds" (as Judas sings in *Jesus Christ Superstar*). Yes, he firmly believes and trusts that this poor earth is not our home. And yet the last thing is only the last thing. We continue with daily tasks, joys and sorrows, and the good that is loving God in this life. Humorously, he suggests to his married friend Eberhard "to say it clearly—that a person in the arms of his wife should long for the hereafter is, to put it mildly, tasteless and in any case is not God's will. . . . One shouldn't be more pious than God."[13] No escapism, no excessive pietism here. We are in the world but not of it; we are attentive to the world but never clinging to it; we trust in a future in eternity, but with whatever time we have here, we do all we can to do God's will.

1 Thessalonians 5:16-18: Gospel Joy from a Distant Land

In various biographies and studies of Bonhoeffer, we discover intriguing moments when Scripture played a pivotal role in his life and ministry even as death was stalking him. The reality of eternity finds its way into joyful life today, as he described things in his trial sermon for ordination in 1930. His text, 1 Thessalonians 5:16-18, spoke of an abiding happiness, one that lasts a lifetime, one that does not dissipate when the happy times are over. "Go and see how children play and rejoice and are happy; see how the birds of the field fly high up to heaven and are joyous in the sun. Watch them, and then watch them again and again, and then rejoice with them, become like them, like a child that is joyous in its father's garden." Bonhoeffer clarifies that this isn't a mood, but an "objective power," one gloriously let loose by the resurrection of Christ. This "gospel-joy" reaches into our lives from a "distant, unknown land."[14]

Marianne, the daughter of Bonhoeffer's twin sister, Sabine, recalls riding in the car with her uncle Dietrich on a day of extreme peril; they were unsure if they would make it home safely or survive once they were home—and yet Uncle Dietrich was leading her and her sister and his friend Eberhard in joyful singing. "During the drive my uncle seemed to me just as I always remember him: very strong and confident, immensely kind, cheerful and firm."

He was always, even to the end, an academic theologian working on high-level, complex projects. If his exuberant singing in the car was any indication, his intellectual theology lived deep in the marrow of his soul. Not just smart religious ideas, but a way of life in the face of many troubles. He didn't get to finish his theological masterpiece, titled *Ethics*, but he left a partial draft, insightful about a great many things, especially "the idolization of death."

He wrote, "Where death is the last thing, earthly life is all or nothing. Boastful reliance on earthly eternities goes side by side with a frivolous playing with life." The Nazis arrogantly believed their Reich would last a thousand years! Off by 988 years, although long enough to leave us haunting, disgusting photos not merely of concentration camp victims, but the Nazis themselves frivolously laughing, drinking, and partying in those hellholes of cruel death. He could see clearly that "mankind is still living the old life," but for the Christian, "it is already beyond the old. It still lives in a world of death, but it is already beyond death."[15]

Philippians 1:12-14: Imprisoned for Christ

What is striking about Bonhoeffer isn't just what he thought about death or his courageous actions that put him at risk of death, but how he died, his final months, weeks, hours, and moments. The story of Christianity is blessed with anecdotes of how nobly various saints have met their deaths. Martyrs boldly professing their faith as the funeral pyre was being set ablaze or as they climbed the gallows. John Wesley, after a long stretch of silence, surprised those watching over his deathbed by singing "I'll praise my maker while I have breath," uttering, "The best of all is God is with us," and then breathing his last. Joan of Arc exclaimed "Jesus, Jesus!" before being burned to death.

We are blessed with his duly famous *Letters and Papers from Prison*, five hundred-plus pages of letters he wrote to family and friends, and letters he received, most smuggled in and out due to the good favor Bonhoeffer enjoyed with quite a few of his captors—a good favor he'd earned by being something of a pastor to them. It's as if we get to sit in his cell with him, looking over his shoulder or out the small window, listening inside his head as he thought profoundly about God and life. It's not hard to imagine his giddy delight in receiving a letter, his only link tethering him to the outside world.

I visited that cell in the Tegel prison by considerable luck. A random visitor to our church, just a week before I was to fly to Germany, was a high-up guy in the German embassy. He learned what I was doing with Bonhoeffer and secured the nearly impossible-to-get visit inside Tegel. After passing through a long series of locked, slamming iron-barred doors, I came to Bonhoeffer's cell. So small, cold, more of a cage than a room. I tried to feel his spirit there with me, with us, and was staggered more than I'd ever been by the personal and theological triumph that was all those letters and papers composed in such a dehumanizing, seemingly godless place.

What we find is something of a miracle. Martin Marty put it well: "From that cramped space designed to kill creativity and bury hope . . . there issued letters and papers that became the substance of one of the great testimonial books of the twentieth century."[16] Thank God his mother, his fiancée, and his friend Eberhard hid his letters successfully—in his mother's case, in her gas mask canister buried at the back of the garden behind the house.

The whole vision here of a Christian in prison writing about God, life, and the church to people he could no longer visit in person is such a Bible thing! Think of Paul writing deeply personal and theological letters to friends far away, and those letters are now books in our Bible, the Bible Bonhoeffer read in his own prison. And how much wisdom has flowed out from behind bars, words that still inspire us, whether from Martin Luther King Jr.'s letter from the Birmingham jail or Nelson Mandela's letters from Robben Island. Or what about Anne Frank's diary from that secret annex in Amsterdam?

Bonhoeffer could be the parade example of something Henri Nouwen suggested as he aged, experienced the deaths of loved ones, and had a brush with death himself. In *Our Greatest Gift*, Nouwen spoke of moving beyond productivity to fruitfulness; as we age, it's less about doing than being. We get fixated on "providing" for our children in the next generation, but it's all about estate planning and life insurance or detailing who gets the jewelry. To be fruitful, you begin now to leave behind what will be of profound personal importance, treasures of the spirit to nurture the spirit. Nouwen names friends who've written letters and poems. Share something that's "you" and keeps sharing that deeper you. I have handwritten notes from my grandparents, and a whittled wooden cross a beloved church member crafted for me the day before he died. Jesus, after all, promised to send the Spirit after he was gone, to be his lingering, powerful presence, more than just memory.

Bonhoeffer was fabulously fruitful with his letters and poems. His tone was upbeat when writing to his parents; he understood all they'd borne when his older brother Walter had died in World War I. With his best friend Eberhard, Bonhoeffer was more candid, complaining about the food, and admitting bouts of loneliness, depression, and cynicism. He maintained his sense of humor. Being sequestered far from the delights of nature, he told his parents that prisoners develop "a very special—probably somewhat sentimental—relationship with animals and plants. Only my relationship with the flies in my cell still remains completely unsentimental."[17] His mentor Karl Barth loved to say that sin is taking yourself too seriously. Bonhoeffer kept a kind of holy levity about himself to the end.

I love his goodbye letter to his parents. "I don't merely want to live, but to do the most I can with my life. Since this must now happen through my death, I have made friends with it also."[18] He'd befriended death from childhood onward. His fresh insight here is wondering how "the most I can do with my life" must now "happen through my death." He's not claiming he will be a modern-day martyr, although some regard him as such. We may well wonder whether we'd be talking about him if he'd made it out of prison safely and lived to tell about it.

Isaiah 53:3-12: By His Wounds We Are Healed

What has moved me, and so many, is what we know about his final hours. Already he'd been like a pastor, not merely to his fellow inmates but also to the guards as well. His fiancée's cousin Fabian was in a cell near him and reported that Bonhoeffer

> was always good-tempered, always of the same kindliness and politeness towards everybody, so that to my surprise, within a short time, he had won over his warders.... He was rather the hopeful one while I now and then suffered from depressions. He always cheered me up and comforted me.... Many little notes he slipped into my hands on which he had written biblical words of comfort and hope.[19]

Very near the end, not knowing whether he had an hour or even a day left to live, he led everyone in singing "A Mighty Fortress Is Our God." He insisted it be sung at an upbeat pace, energetically. I wonder what they all felt when they sang "And though this world, with devils filled, should threaten to undo us; we will not fear, for God hath willed His truth to triumph through us." The day before his death, he was asked to lead a small worship service. His text? Isaiah 53:5: "He was pierced for our transgressions; / by his wounds we are healed." No radical Christianity here. The very basics, trusted in and counted upon during radically agonizing hours.

Bonhoeffer had reported that he had a sense of angels being present with him, no doubt recalling those angels his mother sang to him about at bedtime when he was a little boy. His last letter to his former Finkenwalde students declared, "Our death is really only the gateway to the perfect love of God."[20]

And then the day came for him to cross that threshold. The camp doctor later reported that he saw Bonhoeffer kneeling just as he was taken outside:

> I was most deeply moved by the way this lovable man prayed, so devout and so certain that God heard his prayer. At the place of execution, he again said a short prayer and then climbed the steps to the gallows, brave and composed. His death ensued after a few seconds. In the almost fifty years that I worked as a doctor, I have hardly ever seen a man die so entirely submissive to the will of God.

Bonhoeffer experts doubt the veracity of this accounting. Bonhoeffer was the kind of person who prompted those who remembered him to be expansive or even to exaggerate a bit.

What were his last words? Surely he uttered what he had practiced in bed in the dark as a little boy. Payne Best, an English secret service officer who'd been a captive in Buchenwald with Bonhoeffer, reported, "His soul really shone in the dark desperation of our prison. He was one of the very few men I have ever met to whom God was real and ever close to him."[21] At the last moment, Best reported that Bonhoeffer said, "This is the end. For me, the beginning of life." Many scholars doubt this, as Best wasn't physically present at the execution and hours had passed since he'd seen him. However, Best had said his goodbyes to Bonhoeffer just hours before the very end. I believe he heard these very words.

Isn't it fitting that Bonhoeffer would say this? Or something akin to this? If any of the reports of how he conducted himself and the impact he had on those who witnessed his dying are manufactured or embroidered in any way, I am not troubled. I recall the day I learned definitively that St. Francis of Assisi actually didn't write the famous "Make me an instrument of your peace" prayer. I was dizzy with disappointment for just a moment, and then I realized that he was precisely the kind of person you'd attach to such a lovely, inspired prayer. I'd love to be the kind of person about whom people might mistakenly think, "James probably said this amazing thing. He was like that."

They Die at Home

Where did Bonhoeffer die? We know the answer: in the yard of the Flossenbürg concentration camp. What happened to his body? We do not know the answer. He was either cremated immediately after being hung or his body was one among piles of corpses the Allied liberators found two weeks later; they were buried all together in unmarked graves in a vacant lot in town.

There's a truer answer, though, to the question of where Bonhoeffer died. In Wendell Berry's great novel, *Jayber Crow*, the title character muses over the death of his friend Forrest and others in World War II:

> Their deaths will not be remembered *where* they happened. They will not be remembered in the halls of the government. Where do dead soldiers die who are killed in battle? They die at home—in Port William and thousands of other little darkened places, in thousands upon thousands of houses like Miss Gladdie's where The News comes, and everything on the tables and shelves is all of a sudden a relic and a reminder forever.[22]

Bonhoeffer died back at home in Berlin, but not right away. In the thick chaos swirling around the end of the war that had destroyed

Berlin and its environs almost beyond recognition, those who loved him had no idea where he was or if he was still alive. The news did not reach Maria for two months. She had been frantically searching for him all that time. The news did not reach his parents for three months. Imagine their crazed roller coaster of emotion, fearing the worst, clinging to hope, the not knowing in many moments feeling preferable to hearing bad news.

Of course, the news came. I've stood in Bonhoeffer's upstairs bedroom in his parents' home, feeling near him at his desk, perusing the bookshelves he made by hand, and his clavichord that he played beautifully. The last time I visited the house, though, I lingered in the living room downstairs where his parents must have wept long and hard when their great dread was confirmed. Precious Dietrich was gone.

Early in his imprisonment, he'd composed a last will and testament, leaving various valuables to his six godchildren, eternal (*ewigkeit*) gratitude to his parents, and his most precious things to his friend Eberhard (his library, his grand piano, motorcycle, Persian rugs, and some precious paintings and icons).

Eberhard also had the ultimately fruitful treasure: Bonhoeffer's letters. My favorite among them all, written on Christmas Eve 1943, to Eberhard and his wife, Renate (Bonhoeffer's niece who lived next door to his parents). After some small talk, he shifts his tone: "I should like to say something to help you in the time of separation that lies ahead." The afflicted one, reaching out to be of comfort to the far more comfortable ones on the outside. His counsel to follow is a little off kilter from conventional wisdom, and in a way that brings healing and hope instead of denial and pretending:

> Nothing can make up for the absence of someone we love, and it would be wrong to try to find a substitute; we must simply hold out and see it through. That sounds very hard at first, but at the same time it is a great consolation, for the gap, as long as it remains unfilled, preserves the bonds between us. It is nonsense to say God fills the gap; he doesn't fill it, but on the contrary, he keeps it empty and so helps us to keep alive our former communion with each other, even at the cost of pain. . . . The dearer and richer our memories, the more difficult the separation. But gratitude changes the pangs of memory into tranquil joy. The beauties of the past are borne, not as a thorn in the flesh, but as a precious gift in themselves.[23]

I have shared these words quite a few times over my years as a pastor—in sermons, one-on-one with grieving people, and remarkably in a conversation I had a few years back over lunch with my friend Dr. Richard Lischer, longtime professor of preaching at Duke Divinity School. He was sharing with me his tentative plan to write a book about the death of his son Adam. No easy call—and what to say? And how to say it? Not thinking I was making a suggestion, I mentioned my deep appreciation for this letter of Bonhoeffer's about the unfilled gap. Rick knew the passage well, and it found its way into his lovely, eloquent book about Adam, *Stations of the Heart: Parting with a Son.* This is the one valid test of any wisdom you think you might have about grief: Can it, does it really speak deeply into the soul of one who has borne a devastating loss?

If Bonhoeffer's mother had for many days clutched the last letter her son Walter had sent before dying in World War I, did she hold this one from Christmas 1943, not his last and not even addressed to her, yet his offer "to help you in the time of separation that lies ahead"? I wonder what she made of his hopeful words during the five years she had left to live. I wonder what Maria thought about them. And Eberhard as well. What was the reading of Scripture like for them once they'd lost their beloved for whom Scripture was so very beloved?

EPILOGUE

As I put the finishing touches on this book, I take great hope from Bonhoeffer's confession that "for the first time, I discovered the Bible"—after preaching, studying, and writing on the Bible for most of his life! Poking around into Bonhoeffer's letters, lectures, sermons, and books, I feel I am discovering finally how to read the Bible. I hope you, beloved reader, feel the same.

Imagining myself sitting next to him reading God's Word aloud and conversing about it, I'm sure we would be light years from the common request I get as a pastor: "Could you provide me with a couple of Bible verses to help me feel better?" and even further from that brilliant Charles Schulz cartoon where a young man says to his friend, "Don't bother me. I'm looking for a verse of Scripture to back up onc of my preconceived notions." Bonhoeffer exposes the way I (and perhaps you too) duck, bob, and weave with great finesses to dodge Scripture's simple impact. It's astounding to me the way this brilliant academic felt no compulsion to apply any spin or clever interpretation to the Bible. For him, God was directly present in the plain sense of the Word, just as God wants to be directly present for us. We don't try to import the Bible into our known world. No,

> we are uprooted from our own existence and are taken back to the holy history of God on earth.... We are attentive listeners and

> participants in God's action in the sacred story, the story of Christ on earth. God is with us today only as long as we are there.[1]

And so, every time we open the Bible we ask, "What is God saying to us here? O Lord, help us to hear." We aren't hunting for generic truths we already accept. What strange, surprising, challenging word is here? What is God asking us to do that would matter, but would be hard? Instead of looking for help, we ready ourselves to be told how we can help God. Do we have conversations about the Word with friends or family members? And it's not just, "What is God asking of me?" but "What is God asking of God's church?"

It would be a mistake to isolate Bonhoeffer as a singular marvel, a lone dazzler we admire because he is unique. Bonhoeffer stands before us in the good company of the holy host who have read and acted as he did. We notice him because of his tragic end. But all the greats, all the leaders, and all the unknown, unnoticed but still heroic believers through history who've read the Bible as God's direct presence and summons are the ones who wake us up to what could be.

Let's close by reflecting on two famous examples who survived the Nazi atrocities, as Bonhoeffer did not. Both are Jews who were arrested by the Gestapo and, amazingly, lived to tell about it. Elie Wiesel is often quoted as saying, "If an angel ever says, 'Be not afraid,' you'd better watch out. A big assignment is on the way." We read expectantly and even bravely, watching out for and even eager to hear big assignments in our reading of Scripture.

We recall Abraham Joshua Heschel, the great rabbi who managed to flee Poland in the nick of time. His mother and three sisters were not so fortunate, dying at the hands of the Nazis. His whole body of thought moves me deeply. Much like Bonhoeffer, Heschel wrote that "the Bible is an answer to the supreme question: what does God demand of us?"[2] Our glory is that something is being asked of us. "Our humble answer to the inconceivable surprise of living" is simply gratefulness "for our unearned right to serve."[3]

Indeed, we tend to think our big decision is whether God exists or how to get God to help us. Heschel pointedly suggests that the primary issue isn't "to furnish God with a certificate that he exists, but the realization of our importance to God's design."[4] Do you hear echoes here of Bonhoeffer's "religionless Christianity"? Heschel spoke less of our reliance upon God, but of God relying on us. "To have faith means to justify God's faith in man."[5] "God's dream is not to be alone, to have mankind as a partner in the drama of continuous creation."[6]

God's all over the place, just as God is all over Scripture, asking famous people like Bonhoeffer, Wiesel, and Heschel, as well as unchronicled people like you and me, in large and small ways, not to be religious but to be fully the ones God made us to be—responsible, capable of hearing, growing, and responding faithfully and courageously. God needs good readers of Scripture who are on the lookout for the next way to be doers, not just hearers of the Word, and readers ready to say, "Here I am; send me" (Isaiah 6:8).

NOTES

CHAPTER 1

1 William Faulkner, *Requiem for a Nun* (Random House, 1951), 92.

2 Frederick Buechner, *Wishful Thinking* (HarperSanFrancisco, 1993), 102.

3 Reggie Williams, *Bonhoeffer's Black Jesus* (Baylor University Press, 2014), 5.

4 Dietrich Bonhoeffer, *London: 1933–1935*, ed. Keith W. Clements (Fortress, 2007), 376.

5 Jameson E. Ross, *Bonhoeffer as Biblical Interpreter: Reading Scripture in 1930s Germany* (T&T Clark, 2021), 90.

6 This and the following quotes are from Dietrich Bonhoeffer, *The Collected Sermons of Dietrich Bonhoeffer* (Fortress, 2012), 142, 155–59.

7 This and the following quotes are from Dietrich Bonhoeffer, *Theological Education at Finkenwalde, 1935–1937*, ed. H. Gaylon Barker and Mark Brocker (Fortress, 2013), 909.

8 Dietrich Bonhoeffer, *The Collected Sermons of Dietrich Bonhoeffer*, vol. 2 (Fortress, 2017), 230.

9 This and the following quotes are from Ruth-Alice von Bismarck and Ulrich Kabitz, eds., *Love Letters from Cell 92*, trans. John Brownjohn (Abingdon, 1995), 63–64.

10 Dietrich Bonhoeffer, *God Is in the Manger*, trans. O. C. Dean Jr. (Westminster John Knox, 2010), 20.

11 Charles Marsh, *Strange Glory: A Life of Dietrich Bonhoeffer* (Knopf Doubleday, 2015), 31.

12 This and the following quotes are from *"After Ten Years,"* ed. Victoria Barnett (Fortress, 2017), 20–26.

13 Dietrich Bonhoeffer, *Ethics*, trans. Neville Horton Smith (Macmillan, 1955), 112.

14 von Bismarck and Kabitz, *Love Letters from Cell 92*, 128.

15 This and the following quote are from Dietrich Bonhoeffer, "Who Am I?" in *Letters and Papers from Prison*, vol. 8, ed. Eberhard Bethge, trans. Isabel Best, Lisa Dahill, Reinhard Krauss, Nancy Lukens, Barbara Rumscheidt, and Martin Rumscheidt (Fortress, 2010), 348.

CHAPTER 2

1 This and the following quotes are from Dietrich Bonhoeffer, *Berlin: 1932–1933*, ed. Larry Rasmussen (Fortress, 2009), 473–76.

2 Dietrich Bonhoeffer, *Letters and Papers from Prison: The Enlarged Edition*, ed. Eberhard Bethge (Macmillan, 1973), 156–57.

3 This and the following quote are from Dietrich Bonhoeffer, *Christ the Center*, trans. John Bowden (Harper & Row, 1960), 27.

4 This and the following quotes are from Volker Ullrich, *Hitler: Ascent 1889–1939*, trans. Jefferson Chase (Alfred A. Knopf, 2016), 636–53.

5 Bonhoeffer, *God Is in the Manger*, 28.

6 George Frideric Handel, *Messiah*, "For Unto Us a Child Is Born," quoting Isaiah 9:6.

7 James C. Howell, *And His Name Shall Be Called: An Advent Devotional* (Upper Room, 2025).

8 This and the following quotes are from Dietrich Bonhoeffer, *Conspiracy and Imprisonment, 1940–1945*, ed. Mark S. Brocker (Fortress, 2006), 611.

9 This and the following quotes are from Bonhoeffer, *God Is in the Manger*, 46–57.

10 John Calvin, *Institutes of the Christian Religion*, trans. Ford Lewis Battles, I.XI.8 (Westminster, 1960), 108.

11 C. S. Lewis, "Equality," in *Present Concerns*, ed. Walter Hooper (HarperOne, 1986), 7.

12 Eberhard Bethge, *Dietrich Bonhoeffer: A Biography*, ed. Victoria Barnett (Fortress, 2000), 260.

13 Bonhoeffer, *Christ the Center*, 111.

14 Bonhoeffer, surprisingly, was not present as he couldn't get away from his pastoral work in London. He approved of the work, although he did complain it may not have gone far enough.

15 Joseph Mangina, *Karl Barth* (John Knox, 2004), 4.
16 Dietrich Bonhoeffer, *The Cost of Discipleship*, trans. R. H. Fuller (Macmillan, 1959), 96.
17 Charles Marsh, *Strange Glory: A Life of Dietrich Bonhoeffer* (Vintage, 2014), 302.
18 Bonhoeffer, *Letters and Papers, Reader's Edition* (Fortress Press, 2015), 465.
19 Bonhoeffer, *Collected Sermons*, 165.
20 Bonhoeffer, *Letters and Papers, Reader's Edition,* 465.
21 Jürgen Moltmann, *The Crucified God,* trans. R. A. Wilson and John Bowden (Fortress, 1993), 223.
22 Marsh, *Strange Glory*, 133.
23 Christiane Tietz, *Theologian of Resistance: The Life and Thought of Dietrich Bonhoeffer,* trans. Victoria Barnett (Fortress, 2016), 37.
24 This and the following quotes are from Bonhoeffer, *London*, 401–4.

CHAPTER 3

1 This and the following quote are from Dietrich Bonhoeffer, *Psalms: The Prayer Book of the Bible*, trans. James H. Burtness (Augsburg, 1970), 9–15.
2 Dietrich Bonhoeffer, *Meditating on the Word,* trans. David McI. Gracie (Ballantine, 1986), 52.
3 This and the following quote are from Bonhoeffer, *Psalms*, 14–15.
4 Dietrich Bonhoeffer, *Life Together, Prayerbook of the Bible*, trans. Gerhard Ludwig Müller and Albrecht Schönherr (Fortress, 1996), 85.
5 Bonhoeffer, *Meditating on the Word*, 8.
6 This and the following quote are from Dietrich Bonhoeffer, *Theological Education Underground: 1937–1940*, ed. Victoria J. Barnett (Fortress, 2012), 514.
7 Bonhoeffer, *Meditating on the Word*, 39.
8 Bethge, *Dietrich Bonhoeffer*, 206.
9 Dietrich Bonhoeffer, *Life Together*, trans. John W. Doberstein (Harper & Row, 1954), 50.
10 Bonhoeffer, *London,* 39, 41.
11 This and the following quote are from Bonhoeffer, *Collected Sermons 2,* 116–20.
12 Bonhoeffer, *Theological Education at Finkenwalde*, 134.

13 This and the following quote are from Karl Barth, *The Epistle to the Romans*, trans. Edwyn C. Hoskins (Oxford University, 1968), 7–11.
14 Jameson Ross, *Bonhoeffer as Biblical Interpreter* (T&T Clark, 2021), 65.
15 John Webster, "Reading the Bible: The Example of Barth and Bonhoeffer," in *Word and Church: Essays in Christian Dogmatics* (T&T Clark, 2001), 88, 101.
16 This and the following quotes are from Dietrich Bonhoeffer, *Creation and Fall*, trans. John C. Fletcher (Macmillan, 1959), 67.
17 Tietz, *Theologian of Resistance*, 51.
18 Marsh, *Strange Glory*, 217.
19 Bonhoeffer, *The Cost of Discipleship*, 111.
20 Maggie Ross, *The Fountain and the Furnace* (Paulist, 1986), 80.
21 This and the following quotes are from Bonhoeffer, *The Young Bonhoeffer: 1918–1927*, ed. Hans Pfeifer (Fortress, 2003), 494–99. Emphasis in all quotes are in the original.
22 This and the following quotes are from Dietrich Bonhoeffer, *Ecumenical, Academic, and Pastoral Work: 1931–1932*, ed. Victoria J. Barnett, Mark S. Brocker, Michael B. Lukens (Fortress, 2012), 453f.
23 This and the following quotes are from *"After Ten Years,"* 22–23.

CHAPTER 4

1 This and the following quotes are from Bonhoeffer, *The Cost of Discipleship*, 41–66.
2 Dietrich Bonhoeffer, *Discipleship*, trans. Martin Kuske and Ilse Tödt (Fortress, 2003), 57.
3 This and the following quotes are from Bonhoeffer, *Theological Education at Finkenwalde*, 134.
4 Bonhoeffer, *Ethics*, ed. Clifford J. Green (Fortress, 2000), 80.
5 This and the following quote are from Bonhoeffer, *Discipleship*, 78f.
6 Bonhoeffer, *The Cost of Discipleship*, 99; *Discipleship*, 87n11.
7 This and the following quote are from Bonhoeffer, *Discipleship*, 100.
8 Bonhoeffer, *The Cost of Discipleship*, 125.
9 Tietz, *Theologian of Resistance*, 17.
10 This and the following quotes are from Bonhoeffer, *Discipleship*, 121.
11 Bonhoeffer, *The Cost of Discipleship*, 158.
12 Bonhoeffer, *Discipleship*, 138.

13 Bonhoeffer, *The Cost of Discipleship*, 164.
14 Jeffrey B. Kelly and John D. Godsey, "Editor's Introduction to the English Edition," in *Discipleship* (Fortress, 2003), 8.
15 This and the following quotes are from Bonhoeffer, *Theological Education Underground*, 466f.
16 Bonhoeffer, *Ecumenical, Academic, and Pastoral Work*, 418–19.
17 This and the following quotes are from *Preaching in Hitler's Shadow*, ed. Dean G. Stroud (Eerdmans, 2013), 54–60.

CHAPTER 5

1 Marsh, *Strange Glory*, 17.
2 This and the following quotes are from Bonhoeffer, *Life Together, Prayerbook*, 27.
3 Charles Marsh, *Reclaiming Dietrich Bonhoeffer* (Oxford, 1994), 94.
4 This and the following quotes are from Bonhoeffer, *Life Together, Prayerbook*, 94.
5 Bonhoeffer, *"After Ten Years,"* 24.
6 This and the following quotes are from Bonhoeffer, *London*, 321–26.
7 Tietz, *Theologian of Resistance*, 119.
8 This and the following quote are from Bonhoeffer, *Discipleship*, 236.
9 Bonhoeffer, *Life Together, Prayerbook*, 27.
10 Richard Rohr, *The Tears of Things* (Convergent, 2025), xviii.
11 This and the following quotes are from Bonhoeffer, *Letters and Papers, Enlarged Edition*, 164.
12 It's worth noting that Paul's "do not be anxious" (Philippians 4:6) was written when he was, like Bonhoeffer, in prison and near the end of his life.
13 Bonhoeffer, *Letters and Papers, Enlarged Edition*, 327.
14 Jeffrey C. Pugh, *Religionless Christianity* (T&T Clark, 2008), 52.
15 Bonhoeffer, *Letters and Papers, Reader's Edition*, 464.
16 David Wolpe, *David* (Yale University Press, 2014), xiv.
17 This and the following quotes are from Bonhoeffer, *Letters and Papers, Reader's Edition*, 467.

CHAPTER 6

1 This and the following quote are from Marsh, *Strange Glory*, 3.
2 Marsh, *Strange Glory*, 392.

3 George Santayana, "To W.P.," 1910, https://www.poetryfoundation.org/poems/46002/to-w-p.
4 This and the following quotes are from Bonhoeffer, *Meditating on the Word*, 70–71.
5 Marsh, *Strange Glory*, 387.
6 Bonhoeffer, *London*, 330.
7 Gerhard Lohfink, *Is This All There Is?* trans. Linda Maloney (Liturgical Press, 2017), 152.
8 Bethge, *Dietrich Bonhoeffer*, 38.
9 Bonhoeffer, *Meditating on the Word*, 51.
10 Bonhoeffer, *Theological Education Underground*, 519.
11 *The United Methodist Hymnal*, "Guide Me, O Thou Great Jehovah," no. 127 (The United Methodist Publishing House, 1989).
12 Bonhoeffer, *Theological Education Underground*, 521.
13 Bonhoeffer, *Letters and Papers, Reader's Edition*, 208.
14 This and the following quote are from Marsh, *Strange Glory*, 97.
15 Bonhoeffer, *Ethics*, 78–79.
16 Martin E. Marty, *Dietrich Bonhoeffer's Letters and Papers from Prison: A Biography* (Princeton University Press, 2011), 2.
17 Bonhoeffer, *Letters and Papers, Reader's Edition*, 81.
18 Bethge, *Dietrich Bonhoeffer*, 929.
19 Eric Metaxas, *Bonhoeffer: Pastor, Martyr, Prophet, Spy* (Thomas Nelson, 2010), 499.
20 This and the following quote are from Bethge, *Dietrich Bonhoeffer*, 661.
21 Marsh, *Strange Glory*, 464.
22 Wendell Berry, *Jayber Crow* (Counterpoint, 2000), 141.
23 Bonhoeffer, *Letters and Papers, Enlarged Edition*, 176.

EPILOGUE

1 Bonhoeffer, *Life Together*, 62.
2 Abraham Joshua Heschel, *God in Search of Man* (Farrar, Straus and Giroux, 1976), 169.
3 Heschel, *Man's Quest for God* (Charles Scribner's Sons, 1954), 5.
4 Heschel, *The Insecurity of Freedom* (Farrar, Straus and Giroux, 1966), 67.
5 Heschel, *Man Is Not Alone* (Farrar, Straus and Giroux, 1951), 175.
6 Heschel, *Who Is Man?* (Stanford University Press, 1965), 119.

www.ingramcontent.com/pod-product-compliance
Lightning Source LLC
LaVergne TN
LVHW032100110926
847876LV00027B/209
* 9 7 8 1 7 9 1 0 4 1 6 7 0 *